A LASS UNPARALLELED

A Lass Unparalleled

A PORTRAIT OF **SUSAN FLEETWOOD**

KEITH CONNELLY

Woodfield

First edition, published in 2003 by

WOODFIELD PUBLISHING
Bognor Regis, West Sussex PO21 5EL
United Kingdom
www.woodfieldpublishing.com

© Keith Connelly, 2003

ISBN 1-873203-92-6

For Katherine and Ruth, who love the arts

For the Shakespeare Centre,
with many thanks for all the
help.
Best wishes
Robert Connelly.

CONTENTS

A Note on Titles

'Now boast thee, death, in thy possession lies A lass unparalleled.' Charmian on Cleopatra, Shakespeare's *Antony and Cleopatra* Act V, sc. ii, lines 314-5

'Go Your Own Way' produced by Fleetwood Mac with Richard Dashut and Ken Caillat, published by EMI Music Publishing, Ltd. Lindsey Buckingham, on *Rumours* album (1975).

'Like a fish swimming backwards' was Susan's own coinage, as mentioned in the text.

'But what about me?' is a cry of self-pity from Varya, in Gorky's *Summerfolk*, a catchphrase Susan would echo ironically.

'I'm God's little golden girl' is a sentence she repeated a lot when trapped alone, as she thought, in a darkened and broken-down lift at the National Theatre one day; not a boast, but a rallying cry.

To Russell Davies, of the *Sunday Times*, goes the credit for calling Sue 'An Ocean Liner of a Lady' in a review cited in the text.

ACKNOWLEDGEMENTS

Thanks go the staff of the British Library, especially Chris and Tony in the Sound Archive; the Senate House, especially those rays of sunshine, Anne and Barbara; the Covent Garden Theatre Museum; the Shakespeare Centre, Stratford upon Avon, especially Karin; the Public Records Office; Nicola Scadding, of the Royal National Theatre Archive; the British Film Institute; the Cambridge Theatre Company (now Method in Madness); Sister Delia of the Convent of the Sisters of Christ (formerly the Convent of the Nativity, Sittingbourne, Kent); Robert Norbury of St. James's Church, Piccadilly.

Immense gratitude is due to Angela Watkins, for first taking me to plays in which Susan was performing, before I ever thought I would be writing about her; to Andrea Kelly and Rosamund Connelly, for suggesting that this work was possible. Rosamund also read the disc, and removed many a hideous blemish; such as remain are down to me entirely. Many thanks to Anne Jenkins for her continued encouragement. Cecilia Hocking, my boss at the London Academy of Performing Arts, introduced me to the director, Peter Craze, who led to Sebastian Graham-Jones, who led to Mrs Bridget Fleetwood and Sally Fleetwood, without whom the work would not have been possible.

Others include: Joss Acland, Polly Adams, Kathy Alger, Juliet Ayckroyd, Sara Badel, Francis Barber, Peter Barkworth, Rosemary Beattie, Cicely Berry, Martin Best, Michael Billington, Giles Black, Isla Blair, Madeleine Blakeney, Brenda Blethyn, Diana Boddington, Michael Bogdanov, Bill Bryden, Doyne Byrd, Bill Britten, Faith Brook, John Broome, Lin Browne, Gavin Campbell, Madeleine Cannon, Diana Carter, Mary Chater, Robert Chetwyn, Tony Church, Nora Connolly, Charlotte Cornwell, Richard Cottrell, Brian Cox, Dermot Crawley, Julian Curry, Sinead Cusack, Charles Dance, Sam Dastor, Desmond Davis, Felicity Dean, Francis de la Tour, Judi Dench, Sally Dexter, Richard Digby-Day, Blodwen Doyle, Tony Doyle, Philip Dunbar, Sue Dunderdale, Robert East, Robin Ellis, Peter Eyre, Karin Fernald, Fiona Finlay, Moira Flynn, Michael Fitzgerald, Michael Freeman, Roger Gartland, Sally Gaugain, Sir John Gielgud, Bernadette Gillette, John Goodwin, Peter Gordon, Michael Gough, Nicholas

Grace, Gawn Grainger, James Green, Roger Gregory, Hayden Griffin, Dilys Hamlett, Terry Hands, Terence Hardiman, Andrew Harvill, Duncan Heath, Vivian Heilbron, Allan Hendrick, Randal Herley, Andrew Hilton, Bill Homewood, Gareth Hunt, Jonathan Hyde, James Ivory, Peter James, Barbara Jefford, Martin Jenkins, Priscilla John, Richard Jukes, Lila Kaye, Michael Keating, June Kemp, Ben Kingsley, Sir Eddie Kulukundis OBE, Michael Lattimer, Sally Leaver, Bernard Lloyd, Geraldine Lynn, Carmel McSharry, Dominic Mafham, Doreen Mantle, Peter Marenker, Rosemary Marter, Sara Mason, Roger Michell, Sarah Miles, Richard Moore, Francis Morgan, Cherry Morris, Shona Morris, Bryan Murray, Adrian Noble, Jim Norton, Joseph Roy Parker, Richard Pasco, David Perry, Ronald Pickup, Tim Piggott-Smith, Elizabeth Pursey, Michael Radford, Corin Redgrave, Nick Renton, Ian Richardson, David Rintoul, Tony Robertson, Mary Robinson, Bryan Robson, Struan Rodgers, Norman Rodway, Amanda Root, John Rothenberg, Catherine Russell, David Scase, Paul Scofield, Judith Scott, Roshan Seth, John Shrapnel, Derek Smith, Christopher Strauli, David Suchet, David Summer, Homer Swander, Terry Taplin, John Theocharis, Alex Thomas, Gareth Thomas, Nina Thomas, Paul Tickell, Alex Thomson, Philip Voss, Nigel Walters, Paul Webster, Arnold Wesker, Diana Wickens, Janet Whiteside, Maggie Whiting and Tim Wylton.

Thanks to *The Guardian* for permission to quote from 'Tarkovsky's Other Woman' by Derek Malcolm in *The Guardian* of June 9th, 1987

Thanks also to New International Syndication for permission to quote from:

'Relative Values' by Sally Vincent, in *The Sunday Times Magazine*, January 29th 1984[1]

'Susan Fleetwood: Work as Therapy, by Philippa Toomey, in *The Times Saturday Review* December 21st 1974[2]

---

[1] © Sally Vincent/ The Sunday Times, 1984
[2] © Times Newspapers Limited, 1974

Thanks to Kathy Alger, Bryan Robson, Vivien Heilbron and James Ivory for providing photographs.

LIST OF ILLUSTRATIONS

Susan, Terry Hands and Stuart Richman at the Everyman

Criminals, 1967

Audrey, with Brian Robson as William, Patrick Stewart as Touchstone, *As You Like It* 1968

Marina, in *Pericles* 1969

With Ian McKellan in *The Recruiting Officer* 1970

Portia, *The Merchant of Venice* 1972

Kate, *The Taming of the Shrew* 1973

Rosalind, *As You Like It* 1980

Rosalind, with John Bowe, *As You Like It* 1980

The Burra Memsahib, *Heat and Dust*, with Shashi Kapoor

Beatrice, *Much Ado* 1990

Anna Arkadina, *The Seagull* 1990

Acter 1995, with Bernard Lloyd, Mr. and Mrs. Swander

Acter 1995, with David Rintoul, Homer Swander

Part One (1944-1966):

You Can Go Your Own Way

I.   Childhood, 1944-1962

SOME WOMEN ARE BORN TO BE ACTRESSES just as some men are born to be soldiers.[1] The comparison is apt and true for Susan Fleetwood, a born actress if ever there was one, but one who came from a service, not a theatrical family. She once discussed with Richard Simpson how many actors came from either clerical or service families[2] and came to refer to non-theatre people, with a touch of disdain, as 'civilians'.[3]

Acting and soldiering are perhaps not so far apart as one might think. Both jobs involve tremendous self-assertion combined with strict group discipline. Actors may have to go almost anywhere in the world, at short notice, to work in a team, hastily thrown together under a strange leader, to cope with a situation that resembles an emergency. Soldiers need the ebullience of actors. Montgomery once said that getting on in the army was a matter of knowing how much insubordination one could get away with. Huge personal eccentricity occurs (one thinks of Ritchie-Hook, the gruesome but endearing pantomime figure from Waugh's *Sword of Honour* trilogy). The job is basically physical, calling for enormous stamina. There is a central performance, requiring courage, from which there can be no shrinking. Not all soldiers are battle-tested, but actors have to act to deserve the name. In these terms, Susan was a soldier's soldier, earning respect from all, and then awe and love from many in the profession. She once said that there was a reason why actors seemed so extravagant to each other off-stage:

---

[1] John Keegan's A *History of Warfare*, Hutchinson 1993, p.226. The text runs 'I am tempted, after a lifetime's acquaintance with the British army, to argue that some men can be nothing but soldiers. The feminine parallel is with the stage: some women are fulfilled only theatrically – a prima donna, diva, icon of the photographer or couturier – yet through that fulfilment, embody a universal idea of femininity that earns the adulation of women and men alike. Such adulation is not enjoyed by male actors, however much admired; a stage hero merely simulates the running of risk.'
[2] Richard Simpson, telephone interview 4.4.98
[3] Peter McGarry 'On Stage', *Coventry Evening Telegraph*, 11.4.80

'Our greeting to and embrace of other actors seem excessive. But it is because we have undertaken such risks together, like being in the Blitz. Regardless of how well we know each other, meeting again brings an immediate closeness because we have shared horrors together. It is like a razor's edge.' [4]

Her mother, Bridget, and her father shared an appetite for adventure. John Joseph Kells Fleetwood was often called 'Mike' in honour of his Liverpool Irish ancestry. Born in 1915, he lost his father in the First War. After grammar school, a solicitor's office didn't appeal. He thought about becoming a seaman, then of joining the Palestinian police, a fashionable contemporary career. At the army recruitment office in 1934 they looked at the tall, thin youth without enthusiasm and told him to 'bugger off'. He had caught sight of a poster advertising the Household Cavalry; it was that or nothing, he suddenly decided. For some reason, he was taken on, and served for two tough years, gaining a Jubilee medal for riding alongside King George V's coach in the Jubilee year of 1935. He bought himself out in 1936 and joined the RAF.

'It started as a romantic notion,' Susan observed, 'and turned into a necessity because of the war'.[5] Mike also liked rock-climbing and writing poetry. In 1937 he met Bridget Brereton, then in teacher training for physical education at Queen Alexandra House. She was keen on Greek dance and came to lament the fact that she could never get her children to take exercise as seriously as she did (although daughter Sally takes after her more than the others in this respect). She was also on the lookout for a possible husband; 'And I got a good one!' He had developed into a lean and handsome man. They met at a Ralph Reader show at the Scala Theatre, introduced by a cousin of Bridget's and were married within two years.[6]

The outbreak of war made him especially valuable. He was in Coastal Command, 220 squadron, flying Hudsons. He was flying one out of Thornaby on February 16th 1940 when he spotted the German tanker *Altmarck* in a Norwegian fjord, laden with prisoners the *Graf Spee* had transferred to her. She moved to

---

[4] Her interview with Jane Evers, periodical undiscovered.
[5] Tiffany Daneff, 'Coming Home to Roost in Hackney,' *Sunday Telegraph*, 6.10.91
[6] Bridget Fleetwood, interview 30.10.98

Josing fjord, but a Hudson of 233 squadron confirmed her there. The destroyer *Cossack* found and boarded her that same day, to the cry of, 'The Navy's here!' – but the RAF had made it possible. Mike and Flight Lieutenant Downton made a BBC broadcast about it on February 21st. Mike was awarded the DSO in 1945.

There were so few pilots in 1941, however, that the burden became very heavy, and Mike was sent off to South Africa to help train more of them. It was still thought at this time that the war would be short. By then they had a three-month old daughter, Sally. Bridget decided to try to get out to Africa, by way of India, but their ship, the *City of Nagyar*, was sunk by submarine in the Bay of Bengal, mercifully after a warning which enabled them to get into lifeboats (this too, marks it as the early war period). 'Some Lascars got their heads blown off,' Bridget recalled. The rest made it back to Gurk. Bridget and Sally got to South Africa a year later, travelling by way of South America this time. They all returned to England in 1943, where Mike resumed flying for Coastal Command – Liberators and Fortresses for 206, then 86 squadron. They flew in formations of three planes, reconnaissance and air-sea rescue, for up to eighteen hours at a time. He was a squadron commander by March 1944 and a Wing Commander by August. On March 30th 1945 his Liberator was struck by lightning while investigating a waterspout in case it turned out to conceal a U-boat. There was a blue flash in the fuselage, and the trailing aerial was burnt. It was, he said, 'a scary do'.

Susan was born at St Andrew's, Scotland on September 21st 1944. When Mick came along in 1947 the family was complete. They all had to get used to a peripatetic way of life, following Mike's postings. 'We had to be ready to pack up and go at a moment's notice,' Bridget says. Susan came to refer to herself, with relish, as the 'much-travelled Miss Fleetwood'.[7] She never lost her appetite for it, loving 'the whole idea of freedom, the romantic ideal of taking flight, which I try to do in my job.'[8] She was to have a collection of wooden and mechanical birds. She amused Terry Hands with her drawings of little girls with long plaited hair, flying about upside down; and she would adorn postcards to friends with little sketches of seagulls.

---

[7] Martin Best, telephone interview 10.5.97
[8] Tiffany Daneff, *op. cit.*

'It was a wonderful life,' she said of this period, 'a lovely, happy, unacademic childhood'.[9] In Egypt they went to live in aircraft packing cases on the shores of the Great Bitter Lake.

> *'It was wild. I can remember it very clearly, though I was very young. It was quite dramatic because we hardly ever wore clothes. We really used to run around the beach like natives. My sister, Sally, and brother Mick and I used to collect seahorses in buckets. We dried them and painted them on the wall. We didn't associate it with death, we just thought it was normal, like children do. Then I came back to England and discovered that there were fairy stories about sea horses as if they didn't exist, so one felt sort of enchanted.'[10]*

Like most children, she acted at home in front of the family. She would make herself a 'perfect nuisance', according to her mother, by making them wait and wait until she was perfectly ready and dressed for the part. It was in Egypt that she appeared in public for the first time, at the age of eight; she was a Flower Fairy.

> *'I was a Wild Rose Fairy, the last one to read my piece. I had to say: "I am the English Rose … there is one part of me that is forever England. England! England!" And of course there we were in this parched place, with hardly a blade of grass, incredibly impressive heat, and I remember choking when I spoke those words. Obviously, children cry, but it was the first time I ever experienced that kind of emotion, something that was written down and that was up here in my head and yet was outside me. And I was transmitting that to people…'[11]*

> *' I was an early starter. I wanted to do it when I was eight. I have wanted to do it ever since I knew it was something that could be done … '[12]*

It is interesting that the little patriotic touch, very proper to an RAF officer's daughter, coincides with dawning self-awareness.

---

[9] Interview with Sheridan Morley, *The Times*, 6.9.82, and with Francis Cox, *Plays and Players* June 1968.
[10] Tiffany Daneff, op. cit.
[11] Vera Lustig article *Plays and Players* Feb. 1991.
[12] Jeremy Herbert, interview with Susan *Stratford Herald* 20.8.90

The next posting, in 1953, was to Norway, where they all lived in a log cabin. 'It couldn't have been more different; pristine, white, cold, sharp, crisp. I skied to school in winter.'[13] There she played her first real character part, as Joseph. She got the part 'because I was tall, flat-chested and big-voiced.'[14] Her mother made the rainbow-coloured coat out of coloured patches. 'I remember feeling overwhelmed by nerves which shows what a powerful effect the experience had on me. After the show I asked mother if acting could be a job.'[15] The applause was tremendous. It was not yet clear to her, however, that this was the answer to the question of what she was to do with her life. Not that it was raised as an issue.

The parents never bothered their children with earnest questions about what they were going to do. At that stage, they were very much a family. 'We needed to stick together. We're in this thing, we'll do it together'. This didn't mean that they embraced RAF social life, with officers' wives coffee mornings; Bridget rarely attended. They decorated just one room in each of their accommodations, to make it more homely. While in Egypt, they vacationed in Cyprus.

Schooling was a problem. All the children were grateful not to be sent to boarding school. Bridget had enjoyed hers enormously, but had sensed that it was not right for this generation. 'It's all right', said Sally, coming from overhearing a conversation, 'we're not going'. Frequent removals meant that friendships were impossible. Susan was shy and solitary. 'I don't think I ever quite knew why, but I was very shy, tortured with shyness as a child. I found a way of overcoming it to a degree by being able to express myself as somebody else, and this has been a joy to me.'[16] She didn't have the consolation of reading, that great resource for a lonely child. Attending sixteen schools left her 'practically illiterate',[17] and gave her a dim view of schooling. 'I went to dozens of them and I got nowhere...[18] my education was shot to hell.'[19] 'I was dyslexic, though at the time nobody knew much about that and they thought I was just daft not to read or write much at

---

[13] Tiffany Daneff, op. cit.
[14] Lynne Edmunds, interview with Susan *Daily Telegraph* 17.4.68
[15] Hugh Montgomery-Massingberd, 'Meeting Mollycoddle', *Daily Telegraph* 11.11.89
[16] Liz Gibbs, 'Two Ladies with Long Memories', *Players International* May 1990.
[17] Lynne Edmunds' interview with Susan, op. cit.
[18] Michael Owen, interview with Susan, *Evening Standard* 3.10.75
[19] Sheridan Morley's interview, *The Times* 9.1.82

fourteen. Reading and learning lines is still a struggle, though I have always been desperately determined and at sixteen I got all my O levels by sheer moral determination to win through'.[20]

There are different views of dyslexia: some say that it is in the constitution of the brain, about which we still know relatively little; others, that there are mysterious twists and turns in the personality, and that it is linked to various kinds of creativity; others, that it is all due to bad schooling. Sally got by in the system until she was 16, when she went to art school in London. Sue and Mick faced continual problems. Mick found written work difficult and disliked learning lines, although he could extemporise on any theme and became the articulate spokesman for Fleetwood Mac (seldom the rock drummer's part; usually they resemble 'Animal' from the Muppets). Mick hated institutions. 'I took him to school for the first time, but half way there he screamed and howled and I had to take him home again. It was no good sending him to school. He ran away twice. When it was term time he could come out in wonderful rashes and let the car tyres down. He made work seem silly, and the other kids followed him like the Pied Piper'.[21]

Susan appears not so badly affected by dyslexia as Susan Hampshire, who, as a child, just could not see that c-a-t spelt 'cat'. Sue Hampshire was horrified to see just how much reading an actress had to do, and there was no way to bypass the situation. Ferocious efforts of concentration were needed, creating a dread of the telephone and the doorbell. Susan Fleetwood had to do the same. She was kind to herself when learning a part, she said, working with a tape recorder in the quiet early hours of the morning, about 4am. It was one of life's great struggles. She loved words, but had no confidence in them.[22] She was never rid of this condition.

The family ethos derived from an age of Empire. Everyone was supposed to be independent and productive, to go off and cultivate their own activity, and to report back once in a while. All were responsible for themselves. In some ways,

[20] Sheridan Morley, op. cit.
[21] Susan, quoted by Sally Vincent, 'Relative Values', *Sunday Times*, 29.6.84
[22] Ray Connolly, 'A Childhood: Susan Fleetwood, *Times Saturday Review*,3.11.90

the discipline was quite strict. Mike was a very honest speaker, even when it was to his disadvantage. All the Fleetwoods are straight-talkers and have no apparent fears. Sinead Cusack recalls Susan as someone who hated all the small vices like meanness and hypocrisy. In their different ways, all the Fleetwoods were also endowed with plenty of energy. The word that Mike Newell uses about both Susan and her father is 'rackety'. On the day that he retired from flying in 1958, her father organised a fireworks display and the kids raced up and down the runway on their bikes.

Mick and Sally inherited Mike's adventurous streak most obviously. Mick's career is legendary. As a change from rock music, he was at one stage ready to take up horse-breeding in South Africa. A friend recalls him travelling in Tunisia, and saying he'd like to own a house there. 'But Mick, you do.' 'Do I?' 'Yes. You have a house, and servants.' 'Well, I never'. Sally had five children, to Susan's incomprehension as to how that could be managed, and has converted a large chapel into a very original and commodious house. When I saw her, she was about to go on a sponsored walk in the Himalayas, and she explained how much she loved the feeling of freedom in swimming in the sea. Susan took rather more after her mother in quiet and self-effacement; but the driving energy was there, only needing to be tapped.

When the family returned to England in 1956, they went to live on Thorney Island. In nearby Southsea was the Theatre Royal. One day her parents noticed that in the current programme there was an invitation for anybody, of any age, who thought that they had any acting talent, to come along for an audition. They left this lying around for Susan to pick up, not saying a word. It was her own idea to go along, at the age of twelve, with no training, a poor education, and just the English Rose and Joseph behind her. Of all the strange pieces to read, she took along *The Love of Four Colonels*, a wordy and whimsical play by Peter Ustinov, which one would have thought way over her head. It worked. A phone call came through from the manager, Mr Wren. 'You don't realise,' he told the parents, 'but you've got something really exciting there.' He offered to begin her career there and then.

'My God,' Sue's mother exclaimed, 'what *have* we got here?' They left her to negotiate her own terms with management. Susan's first part was to be Dixie, one of the no-neck monsters in Tennessee Williams' *Cat on a Hot Tin Roof*. She carried it off well, and was offered another, that of Laurel, an English sixteen-year-old in Enid Bagnold's *Chalk Garden*. This precocious child has a good many lines. She pretends to be very knowing about adulthood and sexuality, but falls under the spell of the new governess, who turns out to be a jailbird. Susan would have been rehearsing this more demanding role while performing the first one. Tearfully, she said 'I would not be able to give of my best', and backed out. Her career had had a false start.

The Fleetwoods next moved to Kent, where they tried living on a disused motor torpedo boat, and then an 86-foot ocean-going boat, the *Waveney*, converted to a barge. 'We spent three years on that. It was bloody hard work, cleaning the deck and all that, but when the oil lamps were lit in the evening it had a lovely cosy, olde worlde glow. My room was kind of bevelled, mirrored cupboard, painted eau-de-Nil.'[23] Susan failed her eleven-plus, and the local authority doubted whether they had a suitable school for her. Her parents chose the nearby private Convent of the Nativity at Sittingbourne. It was an excellent choice.

She didn't go for religion. Many fee-paying Anglican children were there. It was originally called the Convent of the Nativity School for Young Ladies. Discipline was apparently strict, but the bark was worse than the bite. Madame Anselm (called 'Annie', but not to her face) presided over all. She was Lady Wingate, a relation of Orde Wingate, the famous soldier. Children stood when she, or any adult, came into the room, and could not sit without permission. Everyone's academic performance was published once a week, and those scoring less than fifty per cent went into detention. There were so many of these, however, that they became rather *blasé* about it.

As a boarder, Susan had a bed, a chest of drawers, and a basin. There was a rota for fetching water, disposing of slops, and having a bath. The austerity of the place bothered her not a bit. On being told that hockey, netball and tennis were

---

[23] Tiffany Daneff, op, cit.

good for her, she played them, although without becoming addicted. Contact with boys was almost entirely banned. Had she met Mick in the street, she would not have been supposed to speak to him. No girl was allowed into the town cafes or fish and chip shop, and if a group left the school, it was in crocodile file, shepherded by a nun, allegedly oblivious of the wolf whistles of the local teds. When boys were admitted to the dancing class, Reverend Mother patrolled with a walking stick, poking boys who got too close. Susan extracted the facts of life from her mother, and reported them back to the others, who promptly took a Bible oath never to do anything so grotesque. Girls are funny that way.

It all sounds like the world of Nigel Molesworth or Jean Brodie – bizarre, but not repressive. Roger Lewis blames Vivian Leigh's convent for giving her manic morbidity,[24] but nothing so dreadful threatened Susan. At thirteen, she was pretty self-possessed. Her contemporary Helene King remembers her 'vividly, tall, with long legs and arms, a well proportioned body, but at that stage flat-chested which earned her the nickname 'Flatwood'. She had a rather big nose, but the most beautiful expressive brown eyes, and her crowning glory was her lovely, shiny, straight long brown hair, held in place usually by a black velvet hair-band. She certainly stood out from the crowd even then. She moved gracefully with her hair flowing back, a very striking figure even at thirteen. Most important of all her attributes was her wonderfully deep velvety rich voice'.[25]

She had travelled much more than the other girls, and could hold them with her stories. Also she knew, after Southsea, that she was going to act. 'Oh, like Audrey Hepburn, I suppose', sister Sally mocked, having just seen *Roman Holiday*. No, Susan meant the stage. On arriving, she told them 'Look, I'm coming here because I want my GCEs, because I can't afford to go to drama school without a grant. I'm going to be an actress, you know.' They fell about laughing and said 'How marvellous, child!'[26] Susan startled the girls by proving, for one thing, that she could weep at a moment's notice. She had a wicked gift for verbal mimicry. There was always the trouble of learning lines, but various girls took turns at

---

[24] R.Lewis, *The Real Life of Laurence Olivier*, Century 1996, pp.129-130
[25] Helene King, letter to author 14.2.99
[26] Ian Woodward, article 'Stars Ascending', periodical undiscovered, 1973.

walking round with her, listening until she had them straight. She made one lifelong friend among then, Rosemary Heyland – 'Mopsy' – who went on to her own acting career at the Central School, and then to become a psychotherapist.

The other lifelong friend was on the staff, Olive Goodyer, Sister Oswald, or 'Ossie'. This lady had taken the veil in 1926, aged 17, much against her father's wishes. Olive was no fanatic, but she was sure of her vocation. She was a liberal, ecumenical sort of Catholic, somewhat ahead of her time. She became a Provincial, co-ordinating the doings of ten convents, some in France and Italy, with the power of assigning staff wherever she wished. For a while she was headmistress at Sittingbourne, but was perhaps not enough of an authoritarian. Reports on her as a disciplinarian differ.

Helene King remembers her as a ' funny scrawny-looking nun with a terrible facial tic, but every subject she taught, she taught with passion and a great depth of knowledge … she was an amazing character, her knowledge of art, history and literature was prodigious.'[27] She took Susan in hand for all these things, giving her one mark for content and another for grammar and spelling. This got Susan through O-levels in English, history of art, drama, European history, geography, biology and religious knowledge, proving that all she had needed was a sympathetic guide. She had saved Susan from thinking she couldn't do anything, making her wish that they had met when she was eight.[28] For her part, Madame Oswald 'knew I'd got something special there … I must not impose anything on her, for fear of spoiling that natural talent: she should not be asked too much, too soon.'[29]

Knowing what a vocation was, Madame Oswald could see it in another. 'Church and Stage – same thing … should be!' Lilian Baylis would exclaim, in words often recalled by Susan's favourite actress, Sybil Thorndike.[30] Some thought Ossie could have been a professional director. She yelled and stormed and threw books about on stage. She insisted on lines being learnt to perfection. She leapt onto

---

[27] Helene King, op. cit.
[28] Ray Connolly, op. cit.
[29] Mary Robinson, sister to Sister Olive, telephone interview 14.12.98
[30] R.Findlater, *Lilian Baylis: The Lady of the Old Vic*, Allen Lane, 1975, p.122

the stage, tassels flying from her habit, beating off the attacks of Tibbs, the school cat, who thought it all a great game organised for his benefit. (Apparently cats think that we are all cats, only too daft to enjoy life as much as they do.) She got parents to help with costumes and scenery, and drew as many as a hundred children into her productions, which regularly won the Festival of Kent prize, and drew glowing reports from education inspectors.

Stella Smith, the P.E. teacher, helped with stage movement, but found that Susan never needed any help. She was, in fact, 'able to restore Sister Oswald's confidence when nothing seemed to be going smoothly, and she let everyone know in no uncertain terms how she despaired of the whole production – a fairly frequent happening which left the whole cast, including the adults helping with lighting, music, etc. absolutely speechless. On such occasions Susan would quietly suggest a movement here, an alternative exit there, or perhaps a piece of music to hide an awkward silence and Sister would continue calmly and peaceably'; Susan just 'had a way with her.'

There was a contretemps during *The Winter's Tale* when Stella, managing the sound, put on a bear's roar when there should have been the crying of Hermione's baby. 'Mighty fine pair of lungs that baby has,' was Susan's remark, which relieved tension. Stella remembers her in comedies *As You Like It, Merchant of Venice,* and as Hortensia in *Taming of the Shrew* where she, 'absolutely brought the house down in the scene where she re-appears with a broken lute jammed on her head. Her distraught expression and air of wounded pride after having gone off so jauntily to 'teach' music to Katherine, stay with me still.'

When they put on *The Tempest*, fifty children formed the waves, and Susan was a great hit, not as Miranda, but as Caliban. 'She almost had to become an animal, her whole body acted. With as grotesque a get-up as could be imagined, was the most savage of slaves, at the same time portraying a monster with clearly human aspirations.'[31] The casting sounds almost as inspired as brother Mick playing Ophelia at his school. 'He was quite, quite beautiful', Susan averred.[32]

She was encouraged to go for a scholarship at RADA. Her vocation had been discovered from within. She hadn't had the chance to get bedazzled by the glitz of showbiz, which, as she came to know it, never interested her. She hadn't been to many plays, concerts or art galleries, but she knew what to do with her life. When she went up for her interview she went in school uniform, brown serge gymslip, cream blouse, brown tie and white socks. Nobody had thought to get her dolled up. When she saw the other girls in shiny tights, high heels and lipstick, she thought that she had wrecked her chance. RADA had long since shed its forties image as a finishing school, however, and although competition was ferocious, hundreds applying for every place, she got her scholarship. She was always to regret not having gone to university. Shakespeare may have felt the same way, but her path into theatre was to be more direct, like his. Mick and she agreed that their parents had been right to let them find their own paths. 'We didn't have to fight,' Mick said. 'We knew what we wanted to do and they said, "All right, go off and do it."'[33]

> 'My parents never tried to persuade me to act. They were so pleased that I knew what I wanted to do. I always had a happy home life. At first I thought it a disadvantage because all the other students seemed to come from fearsome backgrounds, which gave them an extra energy. Mine was so calm and gentle. I felt awfully dull!'[34]

In later life when she met seventeen-year olds who didn't know what to do, she was '...horrified ... I knew so early on ... At sixteen, I felt thirty ... I seemed to know about adult living without having lived it.'[35]

The last statement brings us up with a jolt. She didn't have to pretend to hate her parents – a relief from a tedious aspect of sixties culture. She had travelled a lot.

[31] Stella Smith, letter to author 5.5.1999
[32] Sally Vincent, op. cit.
[33] Sally Vincent, ibid.
[34] Jane Evers, op. cit.
[35] Jane Evers, op. cit.

But what had she felt and understood by then? She didn't have a sense of how institutions work, the RAF being pretty distant from her day-to-day life. Politics and the clash of ideologies never meant anything to her. She hadn't had the chance to have a boyfriend of any sort. It wasn't nearly so common then as it is now to have affairs at seventeen, but Sally and Mick were by this time in London, too, doing what they could to keep off the dull times. It is sometimes useful to work off early mistakes on the grossly unsuitable types that come along, to be ready for better, later. Perhaps none of us play all the seven ages of man with conviction. Susan let childhood and adolescence go, aspiring to early maturity, trusting to her seriousness, her concentration and enormous energy. At this age, she reminds me of Henry James's sombre heroine, Nanda Brookenham of *The Awkward Age*. Contrasting her with a very conventional friend, James says:

> *Nanda, beside her, was a northern savage, and the reason was partly that the elements of that young lady's nature were already, were publicly, were almost indecorously active. They were practically there, for good or ill; experience was still to come and what they might work out to still a mystery, but the sum would get itself done with the figures now on the slate. Both the girls struck him as lambs with the great shambles of life in their future. [Nanda] struggled with instinct and forebodings, with the suspicion of its doom and the far-born scent, in flowery fields, of blood.*[36]

---

[36] Henry James, *The Awkward Age*, Penguin 1972, p.181. Text of the New York edition of 1908; first edition was 1889.

II.   RADA and the Everyman 1962-1966

WHEN SUSAN JOINED, IN THE SPRING TERM OF 1962, the Royal Academy of Dramatic Arts was housed in its Malet Street premises, rebuilt in 1954 after war damage, and under only its second principal, John Fernald, who had replaced Kenneth Barnes in 1955. Barnes's book, *Welcome, Good Friends*, recalls the nineteenth-century spirit of pious endeavour in which it was all conceived, under such guiding spirits as George Bernard Shaw, Arthur Pinero and J.M. Barrie.

During Barnes' reign there had been many changes, due to the individual students admitted, and the kind of chemistry they generated. Peter O'Toole, Albert Finney, Tom Courtenay and Frank Finlay had already passed through and were building their reputations. (RADA's official line has always been that its purpose was to equip students to make a living in the profession rather than to turn out a few superstars, but the big names inevitably spring to mind.)

There was a new intake every term, which gradually increased the social mix. The difference Fernald made was to bring the school closer to the profession, and he recalled the atmosphere as friendly and not especially competitive. In his book *Sense of Direction: The Director and his Actors*, Fernald advised students: 'Never let yourself be affected by what you may think is bad about your fellow students. Concentrate on what you know is good and from this your own good will grow.'[1]

Peter Barkworth taught there between 1955 and 1964 and agrees with Fernald as to how it felt. Although only twenty-six when he began, he had an established reputation and the students respected him. He describes the Dickensian reality that so often appears behind the façade of the most august British institutions.

> [RADA had] 'the most evocative smells of any building I know; a small stone
> staircase down to the little theatre in the basement and as you descend it

---

[1] J. Fernald, *Sense of Direction: The Director and his Actor*, Secker and Warburg 1968 p.189

15

there are whiffs of greasepaint and powder from the make-up room, of musty old clothes from the wardrobe, of cigarette smoke from countless fags smoked quickly in the corridors during intervals, and finally, as you enter the theatre, of canvas and wood and paint from the stage. The larger theatre, the Vanbrugh, has a clean smell, like Wright's coal tar. But the classrooms reek of stale breath and the wood of old tables and chairs. The windows have to be shut because of the deafening traffic in Gower Street, so the smells have no escape except into the staircase and landings. The Canteen at the top smells perpetually of shepherd's pie.' [2]

Peter O'Toole described it as rather like a public school, with forbidden stairways and portraits of the great and good on the walls.[3]

Peter Barkworth was there to teach what was then called 'technique: movement and gesture, then props, doings (laughing, crying, listening, drinking, knitting, etc.), comedy, pace and so on and so on. I used improvisation a lot.'[4] There was the director Judith Gick, whose book, *The Dangerous Actor* breathes a spirit of friendship and openness between teacher and student.

'There was a small hell-hole under the stairs which was known as the staff cloakroom (ladies) where much serious discussion took place on what to do with students and how to do it. After work, some of us would go across to the ristorante in Goodge Street to continue our talk over a plate of spaghetti. There was one staff member with whom I frequently sat talking about acting. She was a splendid actress and a splendid, though terrifying, teacher. The presence of students weeping on the stairs was a sure sign that her class was just over. Minutes later, one would find her at lunch in the staff canteen. She would look up, beam and say warmly, 'They are very talented!' For me, there was a never-to-be-forgotten occasion in the ristorante one evening… when she said, 'You know, my dear, you learn from your students.'[5]

---

[2] P. Barkworth , *First Houses*, Secker and Warburg 1983 p.115
[3] Peter O'Toole *Loitering with Intent, The Apprentice*, Macmillan 1996 p 215-6
[4] P. Barkworth, *First Houses* p.113
[5] J. Gick , *The Dangerous Actor* ,Virtual Angels Press 1997, preface.

Barnes had fears of 'Svengali methods'[6]growing up, which seem unfounded. There was Clifford Turner, embodiment of 'the voice beautiful' according to Madeleine Blakeney. Peter Barkworth remembers him as one of the best teachers, along with Fabia Drake; 'Clifford Turner had a lot of strictness and rules for us in Voice Production Classes, the main one being that we should use a method of breathing called 'rib reserve breathing'.

> *'Rib resahve breathing', I can hear him saying, in his sonorous baritone. We all agreed that Clifford Turner's voice was too perfect for him ever to be an actor, but because we could never achieve a similar perfection, it was all right to follow his methods… He was tall and gaunt and good-looking and we all loved him. He was a lonely man, I later discovered, but there was no sign of that in the classroom. His delight when he saw any sign of improvement made us laugh with pleasure. 'Bettah, bettah', he would say.[7]*

Peter O'Toole recalled him as the 'dearest of men. I picture him now, as a tall, fine head, frank eyes, square powerful frame, fluently beautiful, vibrant voice, chortling wicked humour. Stylish in dress and manner, a self-mocking man, a dedicated and extraordinarily effective teacher.' [8] It is an intimidating experience for the layman, or 'civilian' as Susan might say, to read Clifford's book, or even those by the world-famous Cicely Berry [9] (who later worked with Susan in the RSC) to try to understand voice work. Movement is no less complex.

As with the overlapping field of the Alexander technique, rival schools of thought clash fearsomely. Clearly laymen haven't the slightest idea of how to breathe, move, walk or talk. (At least as an infant one knows how to drink, and that skill, like these others, is capable of infinite refinement.) Yat Malmgren was a luminary brought in from outside, with a movement philosophy of his own, a variant of the Laban technique, which led him off to found his own Actors' Centre.

---

[6] K. Barnes, *Welcome, Good Friends*, Peter Davies, 1958 p.139
[7] P. Barkworth, *First Houses* pp.38-9
[8] O'Toole, op. cit. p.120
[9] See James Clifford Turner, *Voice and Speaking in the Theatre*, Sir Isaac Pittman and Sons 1956, Cicely Berry, *The Actor and his Text*, Harrap 1987, *Voice and the Actor*, Harrap 1983, *Your Voice and How to Use It*, Harrap 1976

Then, like some exotic bird, there was Toshka, a distinguished Polish lady in her fifties, trained in Imperial Russian ballet.

Born Antonia Krazewski, she took the stage name of Maria Fedro from a gypsy family. She had played at the Vienna Comedy theatre and had been principal dancer with the Kurt Joos prewar company. Arthritis prevented her from following up this career. She had married a Polish ambassador and was herself working for the Polish government in Paris in 1940. She moved to England, for obvious reasons, to work at the Opera School, where she was remembered as an 'absolutely invaluable, brilliant personality. The students loved her.' [10]

Fernald brought her in from there to RADA. Terry Hands wrote that she was 'a formative influence on me and inspiration on me and on every student who was lucky enough to be taught by her.' Ronald Pickup wrote:

> '*Because she was European, because of tradition (behind her) she brought something un-English. In drama school, apart from technical skills, you can't learn acting. You can only apprehend what it is. She gave distillation of what great performance is. She was the central part of your life at Rada. Her classes were something you couldn't wait for. She was a life-force.*'

Sian Phillips said that she had an exotic quality set against the drab fifties, when she arrived. 'She was very good at turning clod-hopping girls into seemingly confident young women. She was endlessly kind to students.' [11]

She was a great theatrical eccentric, like Lilian Baylis, whom she resembled in that she was a law unto herself when driving a car. I haven't heard what happened if a student didn't get on with her. Like most charismatic people, she didn't convince everyone. Juliet Ayckroyd recalls her spending half an hour demonstrating one fan movement *à propos* of Restoration comedy, which director Teddy Gray taught as more or less pure fun.

---

[10] *The Times* obituary 16.2.91
[11] Typescript prepared by Madeleine Cannon for the memorial service in Covent Garden church Feb. 1991

Toshka's great admirers, however, included Alan Rickman, June Kemp, David Perry and Madeleine Cannon. They were all at her memorial service at St Paul's church, Covent Garden, in February 1991, along with Susan.

It is hard to say exactly where Susan was in this community. She didn't comment very much on this period, and she remained much of a loner. She made a good friend of Angela Pleasance, who was about the only person invited back to Scarsdale Villas. She phoned her parents almost every day. 'Blinkers on, this is serious work,' was her outlook. 'There was no one ethos at Rada,' Michael Lattimer recalls, 'it's just that Fernald was bloody good at picking people.' [12]

John Broome, the modernist movement teacher, remembers Susan with affection:

> *'I can only describe Susan's action as effortless sculptural flow ... this was indeed the hallmark of her bearing. Few actresses have this ease and restraint to such a high degree. She was a warm and loving person, and this shone through in performance. It also made her completely unselfish on stage. I do not believe there was a single awkward moment in rehearsal; she was generous and open-hearted, and it was not in her nature to make difficulties. I remember her with admiration and with great respect.' [13]*

Her voice was a speaking voice rather than for singing, but John Theocaris has 'one more indelible image':

> *'The Little Theatre at Rada, 1963 ... [Susan] alone on stage, a single spotlight on her, perching on a stool, cross-legged, meditatively strumming a guitar and crooning 'The Moon of Alabama' in a marvellously forlorn, yet stoical, unsentimental voice that touched the heart and has us all transfixed.' [14]*

Susan loved her voice work. Her own teacher was Elizabeth Pursey, who recalls her never complaining about her dyslexia, or even mentioning it. Sue was never

---

[12] Michael Lattimer, interview 6.8.98
[13] John Broome, letter to author 3.1.99
[14] John Theocaris, letter to author 17.9. 1999

one to ask for favours. Nature had blessed her with a fine contralto voice, 'true, theatre-sized, musical, expressive' [15] according to Peter Barkworth, who remembers Susan as 'wonderfully good' [16] in his class. She knew she had 'worked hard, particularly on my voice, and it is very strong. Some actors don't speak from the correct part of their body and when it comes to heavy parts every night they can't keep it up.' [17]

It must have been a relief to be introduced to the full range of acting skills. From watching the established giants of stage and film then, Olivier, Gielgud, Richardson and Donald Wolfit (still John Gabriel Borkman in 1962) it would have been possible to think that acting was all about eloquent declamation. In his book, Fernald described the difference Chekhov and Stanislavsky had made:

> 'Tchekhov's discovery that words themselves hardly matter at all, and that it was what lay between the lines that mattered, was a revelation. It brought the director into being and transformed the art of acting.' [18]

He described one Rada exercise:

> 'The students would sit facing each other very closely and looking into each other's eyes. Each opposing partner would then pour out a stream of improvised and self-assertive dialogue with the intention of matching both the sense and the force of his own words so that his 'meaning' could prevail over that of his opponent. Whoever lost the contest by failing to out-concentrate the other was silenced. The exercise developed the will of each individual, enhanced his ability to centre on a feeling and to keep it strong and true, no matter how great the distraction. No one who succeeded in the competition would ever after fail in attention or power of emotion.' [19]

If Susan ever did this exercise, it is a fair bet that she was very good at it. She was Madame Y in Strindberg's *The Stronger*, a playlet consisting of a monologue from

---

[15] P. Barkworth, *The Complete About Acting*, Methuen Drama 1991 p.97. He compares Susan to Frances de la Tour and Eileen Atkins.
[16] Peter Barkworth, telephone interview 24.11.98
[17] Her interview with Geraldine Ransen, *Sunday Telegraph* 25.7.76
[18] J. Fernald *Sense of Direction* p.20
[19] Fernald, ibid. pp.180-1

Madam X about her marital problems, for which it becomes clear Madam Y is responsible. Madam Y says not one word, but she dominates throughout. John Theocaris recalls Sue in Ionesco's *The Chairs*:

> *'I was full of admiration for the conviction and the naturalness with which Sue gradually assumed the stiff, doubled-up body of the crumbling hag and her demented logic, shrewdly "becoming" the part through her dramatic instinct and natural ability to concentrate and play it entirely from within.'*[20]

Gentleness coexisted with a kind of ferocity in her. Fellow actors at both the RSC and the National were to describe her stage presence as 'tigerish'. Sitting at rehearsals, listening, her eyes would be blazing like a hawk's. And yet Elizabeth Pursey recalls Susan's 'charming reticence, a quality of absorbing everything into her own private timetable of development.'[21] Madeleine Cannon remembers Sue sweeping about the place in a great trenchcoat, with an infectious laugh.

None of it came easy. Terry Hands believes that any actor who totally loses their stage fright ceases to be an actor. At the age of 29, recalling her student days for interviewer Jane Evers, Sue said that she used to go:

> *'...the colour of this lettuce ... and I'm still unreliable. I can be overcome by an uncontrollable terror, for no known reason, as I enter the stage door. I call it my 'horrors'. Sometimes they disappear after a few moments on stage. On other occasions they are with me the whole time and I want to turn to the audience to say 'I'm so miserable up here. Please go back into the bar. You can't possibly be enjoying it.'*[22]

At Toshka's memorial service, when Susan was forty-seven, she told David Perry that stage fright was still endemic. For the time being, however, it was under control. Each year someone shone at RADA, she thought, and that year it just happened to be her.[23] She won the Bancroft Gold Medal, the Forbes Robertson, Emile Littler and Vanbrugh awards, a clean sweep. She was embarrassed at the

---

[20] John Theocaris' letter 17.9.1999
[21] Elizabeth Pursey, telephone interview 15.10.98
[22] Interview with Jane Evers, periodical unidentified.
[23] Ray Connolly, 'A Childhood: Susan Fleetwood' *Times Saturday Review* 11.3.90

number of times she had to keep getting up from her seat at the final ceremony. John Fernald fully believed that she would be recognised as a great actress. At the end of year productions, in which all students could take part, she was both Lady Macbeth and Cleopatra. Some thought that she hadn't quite got the weight to carry those roles off to perfection. (It had to be explained to her that the line 'O happy horse, to bear the weight of Antony' had a sexual connotation.) Ronald Pickup would rather have been Hamlet than Macbeth, but the production was built on Susan's Lady Macbeth.

She took part in the academy's trip to Arizona in the summer of 1964, billed as 'Shakespeare in the Desert'. It was a great honour to be chosen along with Ronald Pickup and Terry Hands, Angela Downs and Nicola Paget. Fernald saw himself as running a company rather than a school. Susan rejoiced that she didn't have to 'think of it like a school, as most people from school do'.[24] Fernald did end up spending a lot of money, which got him into trouble with the governing board, and finally led to his resignation in 1965. This six-week trip, at least, was a happy venture. Five weeks touring in England were added on.

In America they played theatres in Tucson and Phoenix. At the former, with a rich patron, there was a replica of the Globe theatre, with a minstrel's gallery. They played eight performances a week of both *Macbeth* and *As You Like It*. Applause was warm, but Susan at least partly disregarded it: 'They fawned over us because we had the right accents.'[25] She enjoyed the Navajo art, turquoise especially. She was destined to take Rosalind much further, under Terry as director; here she played opposite his Orlando. It was a charming way to advance their affair.

Terry was the first man to interest her seriously. She wouldn't fool around with men, she had told her parents. Like her, he had a service family background, with his father the bandmaster at Aldershot for the Duke of Cornwall's Light Infantry. His mother was German. He had read English at Birmingham before coming to RADA and he had thought of becoming an academic or joining the

---

[24] Her interview with Frances Cox, *Plays and Players* June 1968
[25] Her interview with Lynne Edmunds, *Daily Telegraph* 17.4.68

diplomatic corps. 'That would make some of my colleagues laugh,'[26] he said with a hearty chuckle, years later, with his reputation as a formidable director well established. He was hovering between an actor's and a director's career, but RADA only offered tuition in acting then. Highly articulate, and with a phenomenal memory and grasp of detail, he also impressed Susan as someone completely serious about theatre. He had a shrewd political sense, and had helped his wife, Josephine Barstow, with her career as an opera singer, although their marriage was destined to end in 1967.

Possibly from his mother, Terry had a Continental point of view, that much British theatre was too unserious, sentimental and flaccid. Brecht and Beckett were still avant-garde in those days, and the trail-blazing director was Peter Brook, who now works in Paris. Brook was Terry's kind of director. His *Lear*, with Paul Scofield, came out at the end of 1962. Susan went to see it with Richard Digby-Day. The *Marat/Sade*, which made Glenda Jackson a star, appeared at the Aldwych in 1964. The other play of that year which Susan saw was *Uncle Vanya*, with Olivier and Michael Redgrave. 'She told me,' writes Corin Redgrave, 'how seeing my father at Chichester in *Uncle Vanya* had convinced her she had chosen the right path in life... She came out of the theatre after the matinee, with friends from drama school. She was crossing the car-park and saw Michael standing by a car, waiting for my mother. She described his pipe, his sailcloth blue shirt, the sheer dimension of his personality. And how it made her want to go on acting'.[27] Susan recalled this clearly after thirty years.

At the end of her training, in 1964, Fernald thought that Susan should have gone straight into the RSC. It would not have been startlingly unusual, and most students then still thought in terms of the stage rather than film or TV. She picked up some experience here and there, at the Connaught Theatre in Worthing, for example, playing in Emlyn Williams's *Dear Evelyn* and Michael Brett's routine thriller *Key Witness*. There was some talk of Exeter, but she chose to go with Terry to Liverpool, for a wholly new venture. They were about to invent a theatre.

---

[26] Terry Hands on 'Desert Island Discs' 8.8.81
[27] Corin Redgrave, letter to author 18.12.2000

Terry, Peter James from Bristol, and Martin Jenkins from the RSC had met at NUS drama festivals, and resolved to set up their own theatre. Harold Hobson thought Martin the most promising young actor in the country. Peter would find the actors, Terry would handle Equity and all contractual problems, and Martin would find premises. This he did, with Hope Hall, an ex-chapel then set up as a cinema at 5-9 Hope Street, Toxteth, Liverpool 8.

'The Barcelona of the north,' Terry called the Liverpool of the sixties. 'I'm still using elements I learnt there. I'm very grateful to Liverpool; so are many of us.' [28] 'It was a marvellous time,' Susan recalled. 'The whole city was jumping.' [29] This was not to be the only time that she was to be in at the beginning of an enterprise. 'I like to be in at the beginning of things.' [30]

The Prime Minister, Harold Wilson, liked to remind people that his Liverpool constituency of Huyton was where *Z-Cars*, the TV police series, was set. The series was considered very 'tough' and 'modern' then; nobody who saw it could ever forget Bert Lynch and Jeremy Kemp or Brian Blessed as 'Fancy' Smith.

There were also Ken Dodd, P.J. Proby, Cilla Black, and Gerry and the Pacemakers. The Beatles had by then soared to superstardom. Ringo married Maureen Cox on February 11th 1965, and the group collected their MBEs from the palace on October 26th. The film of *Help* came out. In May, Liverpool beat Leeds 2-1 in the Cup Final. Terry Hands was amazed at the sea of red and white colours created by the supporters, and the team has had his emotional support ever since. (In 1966 they went down to Chelsea, but it was Everton's turn to win the Final, beating Sheffield Wednesday.) The new Roman Catholic cathedral had begun building in 1963.

There was a grimmer side to Liverpool, however. Despite the cultural renaissance, it was in economic decline, although the problems were not yet so bad as Alan Bleasdale was to portray them in the Thatcherite era, with *Boys from*

---

[28] 'The Late Show' BB2, produced Sarah Dunant, 2.11.90
[29] Interview with Sheridan Morley, *Times* 9.1.82
[30] Dominic Gray 'A Fleeting Glimpse', *What's On*, October 1988

the Black Stuff. (Alan was to be closely associated with the Everyman after it was rebuilt in 1975.)

Orwell described Barcelona as a working-class city when he was there, and Liverpool has been so since the war, when the middle class left. It is still quite an eye-opener for a Southerner. The best hotel, the Adelphi, is still not for the faint of heart on a Saturday night. In his book *The Man who Gave the Beatles Away* Allan Williams, their first manager, describes the crudity and poverty of the clubs, and the savage gang fights that would happen from time to time. The Beatles stepped straight from a world of dossing down on planks and borrowing a bob for a chip butty into fantastic affluence.

When Councillor Harry Livermore (ex-lord mayor, 1958/9, and on the board of the Liverpool Philharmonic) persuaded the council to subsidise a fourth theatre, with an outright grant of £3,000 and £2,000 p.a. more for educational work, it was partly to civilise young Scousers. (Later the theatre was to get two shillings per child.) Sam Wanamaker's 'New Shakespeare' theatre had just failed, and the council felt obliged to make a go of this new venture.

There had to be a board to receive the money, so the three founders were joined by Arnold Wesker and John Fernald, among others. Peter Ustinov and Michael Redgrave were patrons. The new place was to be called the Merseyside Everyman. It would only function as a theatre on Mondays, Tuesdays and Wednesdays, not the best nights for audiences. Then all the stuff had to be shifted to make way for beat groups like the Roadrunners and the Scaffold (who hadn't yet risen to the dizzy heights of 'Lily the Pink').

Leslie Blond, the owner of a string of cinemas, including this one, was hoping to launch a rival to the Cavern. When the cinema seats had been removed, the capacity was 700, but the actors had to build the stage themselves. It was called a 'thrust' stage, very close to the audience, and it was hoped that a new style of performing Shakespeare would evolve, to rival the Playhouse. 'I remember Susan Fleetwood and John McEnery going round with bits of wood to fill up the cracks,'[31] actor Terry Taplin recalls. They were both completely cack-handed, according to Terry Hands, whose skills include those of a handyman. 'Couldn't even knock a nail in. Tell them to pull nails out, and they'd happily do it all day'.[32] The spirit was willing. The varnishing of the stage was completed half an hour before the first curtain, and the walls had just been painted. Costumes were run up on a sewing machine balanced precariously on a plank, the flex trailing miles away to a lights plug. During the whole of their time there, the actors had to do everything, box-office, publicity, props, the lot. Equity could have closed them down at any time.[33]

Susan's audition piece was Charlotta Ivanovna in *The Cherry Orchard*, the oddly quirky and unknowable girl. Susan made her very funny, talking abstractedly while slowly taking a stick of celery from within her skirt and biting pieces off. The company was youthful. Two Liverpool actresses, Maureen O'Brien and Alex Stavron, joined Susan. Peter James was twenty-four, his wife Anthea, the wardrobe mistress, twenty-one. Terry Hands was twenty-five, Terry Taplin twenty-four, and Martin Jenkins twenty-five. Martin wanted it to be a centre for ballet, film, opera, beat music, art exhibitions, jazz and poetry. 'Some people believe it is a gamble. It isn't… We are determined and convinced it will succeed.'[34]

There was a civic reception for opening night, September 29th 1964. John Fernald was there, so unutterably depressed that he repeated his advice to Susan to get out and have nothing to do with it all. No, she would stay, and they all threw themselves into the first play, *Henry IV Part One*, with such gusto that Peter James, Patrick Hardy and both Terrys were all injured during the swordfighting, and Martin Jenkins, as Falstaff, collapsed under the weight of his padding.

'At 5.30 p.m. they were coming off-stage … after performing Henry IV *before an audience of school children. By 7.30 p.m. they had taken off their*

[31] Doreen Tanner, *The Everyman: The First Ten Years*, Merseyside Everyman Theatre Company 1974, p.2
[32] Terry Hands interview 17.2.99
[33] Ray Connolly, op. cit.
[34] *Liverpool Post* (hereafter LP) 26.8.64

Shakespeare costumes and make-up, dashed out for a meal and made up again for the Victorianism of Henrik Ibsen.[35]

Susan was Lady Percy, the feisty young bride to Hotspur (John McEnery). Thought by some to be too large for the part, Susan played her as distinctly sexy, but alas her young Mercutio-like husband is more besotted by war than by her. Maureen O'Brien played the daughter to the deranged old Welshman, Glendower (Martin Jenkins). Susan didn't appear in the Ibsen, *Enemy of the People*. This was given a Liverpool setting, not entirely convincing, according to the *Liverpool Echo*. There was at some stage a *Caretaker*, with no female part. On November 2nd Richard Digby-Day directed Goldoni's *Servant of Two Masters*, in which Susan was principal girl. She was judged 'exceptionally good', convincingly disguised in breeches and top-boots, winning 'even when the role requires her to make fun of all the romantic ideals.'[36] It also required her to bare a breast, to prove her sex, whereupon a nun led a row of schoolchildren out of the theatre.

From there, on November 24th, they went on to *Murder in the Cathedral*. As leader of the chorus of women Susan was 'tall and lyrical'[37] and 'nun-like and intense'[38] alongside her RADA colleague, Una Trimmings. They rendered the terror and despair of the chorus convincingly. The production transferred to the Anglican cathedral. Terry had chosen to do it, remembering a great RADA success, but when he sat down to read it, he found not single idea on how to interpret it. He sat up all night, reading it over three times. He concluded that they could do it as 'not a play at all … a ritual vindication of God's pattern … there is no allowance for the presence of the actor'.[39] This bears most against the actor playing Becket, and Stuart Richman did not see eye to eye with Terry. There were some fierce disputes between Michael, Martin and Terry as to which plays to do and how to do them, lasting into the early hours of the morning. Martin and Stuart were shortly to leave. Terry, the Wunderkind, usually got his

---

[35] D. Tanner, LP 6.10.64
[36] D. Tanner *Liverpool Echo* (hereafter LE) 3.11.64
[37] P. Fiddick, LP 25.11.64
[38] D. Tanner LE 25.11.64
[39] Terry Hands 'Producer's Note' (the word was interchangeable with 'director').

way. Oft clad in black, and eating cold baked beans for breakfast, he was creating a persona almost as definite as the Elizabethan villain. In those days he sported a small beard, making him look like a young Viking. (My fantasy for him as an actor is as a replacement for Robert Shaw, as Colonel Hessler, the panzer commander in *The Battle of the Bulge*.)

On January 11th 1965, Peter Fiddick of the *Post* wrote that, 'In the first 11 weeks of the Everyman's existence, 15,261 children went to the afternoon performances. In the 12th week a record 2,491 saw the show ... some kids went back in the evening ... Many of them have even declared a switch of affection from the 'Stones' to members of the Everyman.' Part of that was schoolgirls, bedazzled by the male stars in their tights. It was presumably not (just) this that made Terry Hands say:

> *'I really feel that I could stay here forever. I just don't want to do anything else... Over Christmas I held auditions in London, and had fifty applicants from whom to choose three men and three women – even though we are paying at the most eleven pounds ten shillings a week and have to clear our dressing rooms on Wednesday night to make way for the beat groups.'*[40]

Terry Taplin gave up work on Broadway, USA, at £100 per week, to be at the Everyman. 'It was the best time of my whole career.'[41] This was despite the kids stealing soap, smashing the lavatories and cutting up rough during *Macbeth*, possibly overstimulated by the drunken porter and the murders. Susan's dressing room was the boiler room. It was still, as Fernald had said, a fleapit.

The Importance of Being Earnest opened on January 25th, with Sarah Buchan as Lady Bracknell and Susan as a 'quite fascinating' Gwendolen, 'a really delightful portrait'[42] 'formidably sophisticated.'[43] On February 23rd she re-emerged as Lady Macbeth, directed by John Russell Brown. She ranged:

---

[40] P. Fiddick, LP 11.1.65
[41] D. Tanner, *The First Ten Years* p.12
[42] H.W.R., LE 26.1.65
[43] D. Tanner LP 27.1.65

'from the gleefully wicked to the insanely, pitifully hysteric … a remarkable achievement. It is positively easy for her to dismiss Macbeth at the start of the play: he recoils from her first greeting almost in horror. She is careful to show the gradual breakdown of the character's resolution, and in the sleepwalking scene she produces the genuine pity and fear. If the rest of the cast came anywhere near Susan Fleetwood this would be a production to remember. In fact, Terry Hands' Macbeth is, while dwarfed by Lady Macbeth (which is as it should be, at least in the earlier scenes), not at all a bad attempt.' [44] The Guardian *reviewer thought 'Macbeth himself was a superficial character, all show and little thought. Terry Hands ranted enough, but there was nothing else to him … Susan Fleetwood's Lady Macbeth, on the other hand, was so powerful and sensitive that one longed for an equal partner. She brought a force of sensitivity to the part which was overwhelmingly effective and the scenes came alive when she was on stage. Her sleep-walking was more horrific than any amount of blood.'* [45]

Terry was quite shaken by this; it may have helped him decide to pursue a career as a director. *Waiting for Godot* and *Look Back in Anger* were interwoven with *Macbeth*. Susan was Alison to Terry Taplin's Jimmy Porter. 'Miss Fleetwood possesses that most precious of theatrical gifts, perfect timing. Her whispered responses to Porter's … verbal fireworks continually riveted attention to her.' [46] She showed 'an intensity of love and an inability to do anything about it which has a strong and moving beauty. Alison has a Home Counties touch, mockingly overlaid by a defensive cynicism.' [47]

In April Peter Fiddick interviewed Susan, calling her the 'unofficial leading lady' of the company.

P.F.	*Would you put your daughter on the stage?*
S.F.	*I'm going to have sons.*
P.F.	*Oh! No, seriously.*

---

[44] D. Tanner, LP 25.2.65
[45] Anne Shearer, *Guardian*, 24.2.65
[46] J.R.C. LE 23.3.65
[47] Anne Shearer, *Guardian*, 2.3.65

S.F.	*Well, only if she didn't give me any competition.*
P.F.	*Do you have any, now?*
S.F.	*No.*
P.F. (shocked)	*No competition?*
Sue.	*No… fool! No daughters.*

She still found acting strange.

> *'You know, sometimes I sit in front of the mirror, in our dressing room,*
> *making up, and I wonder what on earth I am doing, plastering all this stuff*
> *on my face, and going out there to speak someone else's lines. It's absurd, isn't*
> *it? But I chose it!'*

She had no actressy persona … 'people not in the theatre expect a certain image of an actress. So you go right against it and do all sorts of different and outrageous things because it infuriates you that they should have a set image of you and not of a typist.' 'I don't think that I would have the energy to put on an act off-stage', for 'acting intrudes into every part of your life. Everything that happens is building up into something you are going to use on stage.'[48]

Fiddick described the company as serious, 'almost frighteningly self-critical, and dead against personality cults.'[49] She didn't have much time to do outrageous things. They all got out now and again to go to the Blue Angel and Jacaranda clubs (still there) and to the Ship pub for poetry readings. There wasn't much money. The cleaner, Blodwen Doyle, was invaluable for her 'Scouse' stew and sandwiches. Harry Livermore always advised them to keep her on, no matter what other staff changes were made, and Susan was always fond of her. 'Just tidy up a bit, Blod' she would say, looking at the half ton of coke with which she shared her 'dressing room'. The actors would go down to Cooper's Hall for leftover food, or go for a Chinese if funds allowed. A bus ride down the river took them to Thurstanton, for a breath of air. Otherwise life was lived in that quarter, of the theatre and the cathedrals. Susan's flat, in Falkener Street, was a short walk away, so company meetings were held there.

---

[48] P. Fiddick, 'Mrs. Worthington's Daughters' LP 14.4.65
[49] P. Fiddick, LP 13.4.65

In May she appeared in Punch and Judy costume opposite Bruce Myers, in Arrabal's *Orison*, a short play, in which they present a couple who recite Bible stories and wonder about becoming Christian, but hanker after their habitual lives, murdering people and picking out the eyes of corpses. Next month she re-appeared as the much more fetching Polly Garter, in *Under Milk Wood*. She had trouble with the Welsh accent, according to Doreen Tanner, but 'still stole some of the honours for a lush yet wistful portrait.'[50]

The company was in continual financial peril. In February students on rag week had given the theatre a lick of maroon and grey paint, making it 'almost cheerful'.[51] One thousand pounds had been raised by an appeal in May, and Harry Livermore persuaded the council to stump up £2,678 in June, to help them look for better premises; they did not materialise. To prove their allegiance to the local community, Terry Hands directed a play about immigration, called *Jack of Spades*, as part of a Commonwealth Arts Festival. Mona Harmond, a black actress, appeared. The National Front took exception to all this and smashed the glass over photos outside the theatre.

The play got a lukewarm reception. *Arms and the Man* opened on October 11th and then, on October 18th *Four Seasons* by Arnold Wesker, with just Susan and David Bailie as Beatrice and Adam, the only characters. Wesker wrote in a heightened, lyrical style, with the risk that it would sound like a recitation. The two lovers live through four seasons, their emotions altering with them, although not predictably. The play avoids banality, and Wesker has no axe to grind about social issues. Adam says, 'Not all the great causes in the world can stop me crying for a passing love.' Both of them feel their limitations as lovers. 'Teach me to love myself', Beatrice says. She resents his good humour, and is alarmed by his making a strudel in summer, although it is an offering to her. She rages at him for not giving her enough attention, and wants him to be a leader of men, like her previous lover. He tries to talk her down from this manic level of demand, but has only managed to fight her to a standstill by the end. There is some hope; it is winter, and he is trying to make a fire for her. Susan gets to play quite a

---

[50] D. Tanner, LE 24.6.65
[51] D. Tanner, *The First Ten Years*, op. cit. p.15

daunting heroine, of many moods. Doreen Tanner thought that they carried a 'melancholy, rather weary theme to its limits of liveliness … they flirt, play, quarrel with all the energy they have. A lot of the time they succeed. But Susan Fleetwood is a little in danger of relying too much on her very clever movements.'[52] Terry thought it a fine play, like a piece of music, but Wesker was annoyed with him for mounting on orange-boxes a play he regarded as essentially sensual.

A pair of queens followed for her, the first a comic one in *The Three Musketeers*, 'a very rich study' wherein she 'literally quivered with suppressed passion'.[53] The second was Shakespeare's Queen Margaret, in *Richard III*. She made 'rich play' of her cursings.[54] Terry directed Bruce Myers as Richard and John McEnery as Hastings. On November 20th Peter James directed *A Christmas Carol*. Susan played Emma Fezziwig, who might have married Scrooge in his twenties, and thus saved him. Doreen Tanner called it 'slight, but pleasant'.[55] At the end of the year, the *Echo* said the company was achieving 'miracles on a shoestring'.[56]

In January 1966 they put on Beckett's *Krapp's Last Tape* and *Endgame*. In February schoolchildren were let in to see rehearsals and at last the beat groups were cleared out. The ever-helpful Harry Livermore got them £900 from the council. Timings were tight; Harry had to sign one cheque from within his Turkish bath. At that time the Cavern Club was £10,000 in debt, and some called for money to go there rather than to a theatre, but it was the rock venue that closed. On February 17th they put on O'Neill's *The Great God Brown*, for only its second British performance.

Susan played Margaret, a seventeen-year old girl at the beginning, a mother of three boys by the end. She is in love with Dion, her husband, an architect of vast imagination, who somehow cannot cope with life. Like many an artistic hero in American drama and fiction he drinks too much, is sexually irregular, bitchily

---

[52] D. Tanner, LP 20.10.65
[53] Ray West, LE 9.11.65
[54] Ray West, LE 30.11.1965
[55] D. Tanner, LP 22.12.65
[56] Ray West, LE 31.12.65

arrogant and consumed with self-pity. He dies, but his rival, Brown, a regular guy, can only win Margaret by pretending to be Dion. In this persona, he is understood at one point to have killed Brown, and so gets himself shot by the police. Dion has triumphed from beyond the grave. Margaret's dialogue remains unflinchingly melodramatic. 'My lover! My husband! My boy! You can never die till my heart dies! You will live for ever! You are sleeping under my heart! I feel you stirring in your sleep, for ever under my heart!' The acting must have been good for the *Post* to call it 'gripping and frightening'.[57]

On March 16th, Michael Bogdanov put on Moliere's *Hypochondriac*, in a 1920s setting, and with his own translation. Susan was Toni, the maid. She was deliberately chosen for being far too big, physically, for the part, and the resultant comedy was fine. She showed a 'flapper-like relish' for the role, with a 'devastating Miriam Karlin accent'.[58]

In April there were articles and TV programmes about the Easter Rising of 1916, so O'Casey's short piece *Shadow of a Gunman* was staged, with Susan as Mrs Grigson, a lady in her forties, married to a blustering, drunken Orangeman. She provides a chorus of lament, most pointedly for the death of Minnie Powell, a girl of twenty-three, all too ready to sacrifice herself for the foolish, posturing men who flirt with trouble and leave bombs about. Arrested for hiding the bomb, she tries to escape from the lorry and is shot 'through the buzzum'. The *Echo* thought that the cast had too much fun with the accents, and that the play really only amounted to 'a pantomime'. Susan 'tries to give the event its true impact with a fine display of grief'.[59]

On May 4th she appeared in the most complete victim part possible, as Lis in *Fando and Lis* by Arrabal, the Spanish exponent of the Theatre of Cruelty. She is a cripple, chained to her pram by Fando, her companion, who beats her and handcuffs her. He also expresses affection by beating a drum and singing a song about a feather. Three men come on, Namur, Mitaro and Toso, and Fando invites them to stroke and kiss Lis. After he has beaten her to death, one of them

[57] H.B. LP 18.2.66
[58] Ray West, LE 17.3.66
[59] LE 12.4.66

pulls her tongue out. All four men then start out for Tor, a project long discussed. This must be the worst play she ever appeared in; not one of Terry's good ideas.

On May 13th there was a major policy review. The government's new Selective Employment tax was bearing hard on theatres, so five actors and half the backstage staff had to go. In June the Arts Council gave £27,000 to the Liverpool Playhouse, but nothing to the Everyman. Terry Hands, Peter James, Gloria Parkinson, Bruce Myers, Brian Walton remained, with the 'indispensable and increasingly versatile' Susan Fleetwood.[60] They resolved on small plays, and no more avant-garde for a while. Charles Dyer's *Rattle of a Simple Man* has only three parts, including Percy (Brian Walton) a forty-one year old schoolteacher and football fan who gets involved with Cyrenne (Susan), a tart with a heart of gold (the cliché is in place). She fantasises about a better life with him and resists the attempts of her brother Ricard (Bruce Myers) to bring her back to the family.

Susan wore 'a skirt fully four inches above the knee' (newly fashionable then) and took off her dress to prance about 'in the scantiest of black undies. Miss Fleetwood employs every trick in the book to keep our attention [whatever else was needed?] ... this prevents us looking too closely at the plot ... she manages to breathe life into the plot and make the most of its occasional funny lines. Some of her sarcastically throwaway remarks are wickedly sharp.' [61]

This says much for her, for she really disliked the part. Her last performances at the Everyman were in June, as Estelle, the smouldering, jealous, man-hungry woman among the damned in Sartre's *In Camera*. The theatre closed on July 17th, to re-open on September 28th with Peter James as artistic director. Terry Hands had been disappointed in expectations of new premises and thought it time for a break. He and Susan moved on to the RSC. The Everyman was to have a chequered career, rebuilding in 1975 and relaunching in 1994 as the New Everyman. One late-sixties fashion was to resent being tied to a building and reverting to the idea of becoming strolling players (albeit motorised, in a lorry).

---

[60] LP 20.5.66
[61] LP 27.5.66

With her difficulty in learning lines, how did she ever cope with this orgy of work? I do not know if any company could put on more plays, or a wider variety, in that space of time. A larger company with administrative back-up, like the RSC, would necessarily go slower. 'We were all incredibly dedicated,' Terry Taplin said. 'We did nothing else, but what we were doing at the theatre. All we had to live for was going in for that day's rehearsal ... The first two years we just ploughed on. To us it was good thing, after good thing. It had to be, otherwise you could get very depressed. It was just total.' [62]

Susan recalled having 'worked myself silly but playing leading parts all the time.' Sometimes they would not bother to go home, but sleep over at the theatre for only three or four hours. 'You can only work so hard and with such total commitment once in a lifetime ... We lived in squalor ... We paid ourselves £7 a week. The firemen got £15 a week ... I think I was the only woman who stuck it because it was pretty tough, and we were working extraordinary hours – just working on adrenaline and emotion ... after two years we began simply to get too old to go on living like drama students. [63]

Susan's first Spotlight photo shows her youthful good looks, with a slightly wistful, long-haired, Pre-Raphaelite look, that still allows for the underlying toughness. She was tall, loose-limbed, coltish, and still with an air of innocence and vulnerability. She was felt to be highly strung; she would burst into tears if, after repeated efforts, it was still not going the way she wanted, but the rage of frustration was never vented on anybody else. People knew to leave her alone just before she was going on stage. She liked a pool of silence and concentration about her, from which she would burst forth with enormous energy. Tony Pedley said that the whole company was in love with her. Stuart Richman says she was called 'the queen'. She and Terry were decidedly an item, and other advances to her were turned away with a laugh.

---

[62] D. Tanner, *The First Ten Years*, op. cit. p.12
[63] Her interview with Geraldine Ranos, *Daily Telegraph* 25.7.76, with Liz Gibbs 'Two Ladies with Long Memories' *Players International*, May 1990, with Ray Connolly's op. cit., with Philippa Toomes, *Times* 21.12.74, and with Sheridan Morley, op. cit.

This must have been one of the happiest periods of Susan's life. She had got in with her comic audition piece, and so many of the parts she played were sheer fun. She found the right touch for them all, and was never accused of turning in a weak performance, or even of appearing to struggle with the part. Although she continually played leading parts, her sense of realism made her think of this as just extended training. She did not want her family to come and see her. 'Come on, Sue' they grumbled, 'you've been at it for long enough now.' Her mother, with Machiavellian cunning, booked tickets to see *Look Back in Anger* under the name of Mr and Mrs Smith. She and Mike watched in alarm as she wielded the flat-iron. 'She can't iron!' It didn't matter, of course, as Jimmy shortly knocks it over and burns her with it. Terry reckoned it one of the very best performances of her whole career.

She had never had to carry the proverbial spear, and work her way up through the ranks, but she was a big fish in a small pond. Now, at twenty-two, she was launched, at a high level, into the Royal Shakespeare Company.

Part Two (1966-1975):

Like a Fish Swimming Backwards

III.   The Royal Shakespeare Company, 1966-1969

ON JOINING THE RSC, TERRY HANDS INHERITED from Michael Kustow the responsibility for running Theatregoround, a missionary project to take plays to inaccessible venues, with a limited number of young actors. 'Gigs, that's what they were', Susan recalled, 'in schools, village halls, church halls with terrible echoes, three or four in the audience – you didn't know sometimes what you'd find.'[1] Schoolchildren came along in the afternoon, adults in the evening, so there was a close continuity with what she and Terry had been doing at the Everyman. In 1966-7, they performed *The Dumb Waiter, The Hollow Crown* (of which more later), a tiny *Henry V,* and two shows involving Susan: *The Proposal* and *Under Milk Wood.*

The first of these, performed in September 1966, is a hilarious Chekhov playlet. Landowner Lomov visits neighbouring landowner Chubukov to ask for his daughter's hand in marriage. She comes in and conversationally she and her suitor stumble on the topic of some meadows of disputed ownership. A furious row develops and Lomov stalks out. On learning that he came to propose, Natalya throws a fit. He is brought back and everyone wants to appear grandly generous about the meadow, while obviously clinging to their first opinions. They then discuss the merits of their dogs and again flash into a blazing row. Lomov collapses. 'My shoulder's come off ... where's my shoulder? ... I die ... A doctor!'

Chubukov tries to revive him, but fails. 'He's dead, and all that... I am the most unhappy of men!'[2] He does revive, however, and is instantly betrothed. As the couple are about to begin a third argument, Chubukov yells for champagne. The lovers, who have not exchanged one tender word, will have their marriage, but it will be a very noisy one.

---

[1] Philippa Toomey, 'Susan Fleetwood: work as therapy', *Times Saturday Review,* 21.12.74.
[2] Anton Tchekoff, *Six Famous Plays,* transl. J. West, Marin Fell, Gerald Duckworth and Co Ltd and Charles Scribner's Sons 1958, p.330

Susan, as Natalya, would have had to yell, weep, collapse, weep and yell again, in quick succession. Terry Hands described the production as a kind of 'open rehearsal'. It was played in three ways, simple, elegant and clownish. Audiences were asked which they preferred. Translations differ, but most read as though the third approach were best. There is strong testimony to the contrary, however. Richard Moore, who came into the piece in April 1967 with Hugh Sullivan, to replace Donald Burton and Tony Church, recalls an evening when (on invitation), a very old lady piped up from the audience to say that she had seen it in Chekhov's lifetime, in St. Petersburg. 'How was it then?' they asked. 'A lot quieter,' was the reply. They were nonplussed: 'It was rather like being confronted with an original spectator to *Twelfth Night*.' [3]

In June 1967 Terry directed Susan, Sheila Allen, Peter Geddis, Peter Gordon, Richard Moore, Bruce Myers and Hugh Sullivan in *Under Milk Wood*. Douglas Cleverdon, who had directed the famous radio version, thought that his Edinburgh Festival production had been mistaken in trying to do it naturalistically, on stage, with over twenty actors. Terry thought that the rather heavily middle-aged characters did not emerge very sympathetically from such a presentation. It was better to concentrate on language, as they were doing in their voice classes back at Stratford, functioning as a language company.

The lines were shared by flicking them quickly back and forth, to 'free the text' and make one forget who precisely was delivering them.[4] Susan enjoyed her parts. 'I used to call her Olive Oyl' said Richard Moore. 'She was as mad as a hatter and brought the most wonderful idiosyncratic energy to whatever she did.' One night she was ill, and Richard and Emrys Jones had to read her parts. They swore to her that they had done them wonderfully, but when she asked to hear them read again, she made wickedly gleeful fun of them, which they took in good part; they had indeed not been a patch on her.[5]

In 1967 Peter Hall was coming to the end of his reign in the RSC. Trevor Nunn took over in January 1968, although they worked in tandem until the summer.

---

[3] Richard Moore, phone interview 10.4.99
[4] Radio discussion on Theatregoround, *Under Milk Wood* and *Hollow Crown* 6.3.68, T. Hands and others.
[5] R. Moore, letter to author 8.9.1997

Nunn was to direct Susan in her first major role, as Amanda in Vanbrugh's *The Relapse* (Aldwych 1967). Recent RSC triumphs had included Vanessa Redgrave's Rosalind (1961) and Peggy Ashcroft as Margaret in John Barton's epic *Wars of the Roses* (1963-4). Glenda Jackson had gone on from Charlotte Corday to Ophelia in 1965, played so abrasively that some critics thought she should have taken Hamlet. Helen Mirren had appeared in Nunn's acclaimed *Revenger's Tragedy* in 1966, and next year Estelle Kohler appeared as Juliet, and Janet Suzman as Kate in the *Shrew*.

Peter Hall had re-interpreted Shakespeare's histories in the light of modern politics, saying that power-playing hadn't changed that much over the centuries. He had inherited the Cambridge tradition of strict attention to the text, with a 'dry, cool, intellectual' style of verse delivery.[6] Ian Richardson and Richard Digby-Day think this was the golden age of RSC verse-speaking. Susan was not chosen for the history plays or the Theatre of Cruelty.

She and Terry became friends to John Barton and his wife Anne, the Renaissance scholar. Susan took his verse-training very seriously. She appeared in his workshop of 1979, televised as *'Playing Shakespeare'* (LWT 1980, Channel 4 1984 and published 1984). Some accuse Barton of heavy pedantry – 'watch those line endings – observe the caesura'. 'When do I breathe?' Ben Kingsley asks at one point.

When Susan arrived at the National, Peter Hall thought that she and Ben Kingsley had 'the same habit of over-emphasising individual words. It's *explaining* the text rather than *being* it.' (Entry[7] of March 8, 1977) He thought this an RSC mannerism. Reviewers don't mention it as spoiling Susan's early RSC appearances.

Susan joined Janet Suzman for *The Relapse*, a piece of Restoration fun, albeit with a touch of Chekhovian melancholy. Susan was Amanda, the faithful young wife to Loveless, a man who thinks he owes it to himself to try the pleasures of the town in the shape of Berinthia, Amanda's cousin, played by a 'temptingly

---

[6] Sally Beauman, *The Royal Shakespeare Company: A History of Ten Decades*, O.U.P. 1982 p.268
[7] Peter Hall, *Diaries*, ed. John Goodwin; Hamish Hamilton 1983 p.287.

vivacious'[8] Janet Suzman. Alan Howard, who according to Terry Hands would have made the ideal leading man to Susan, was in the play, but appeared in the subplot, as Young Fashion, an open-hearted young man who outwits his brother, Lord Foppington, and steals his bride-to-be. This foolish new-made lord (Donald Sinden) clumsily assails Amanda, who promptly slaps his face. Later, Amanda is distinctly tempted by a superior specimen, Worthy. There was 'steamy sexual excitement' in his attempted seduction scene.[9] She summons her resolve, in verse, on behalf of her unworthy husband:

> 'My forces rally bravely to my aid
> And thus I gain the day ...'

Thus the difficult transition in which she passionately rejects her lover becomes a moment of piercing, unexpected gravity. No wonder it leaves Worthy – 'played by Patrick Stewart with engaging fruitiness – uplifted in a rapture'.[10] Alas, Vanbrugh did not write a follow up scene in which Amanda confronts either Worthy or Loveless, who never has to admit his infidelity; the subplot takes over. Recalling her part in later years Susan called Amanda '...a dull little mouse. I didn't have the courage then to do anything with it ... When you are acting what seems to be a boring character then one's got to be fairly resourceful to avoid being actually boring to the audience.'[11]

The reviews were much kinder to her than she was to herself. 'Susan Fleetwood shares in every nuance of fascination and dismay as Amanda puts a cautious toe into the treacherous waters of adultery.'[12] She was 'primly inviolate', 'virtue personified', 'a tiny and astoundingly true center of beleaguered virtue', displaying 'touching vulnerability'.[13]

---

[8] Milton Shulman, *Evening Standard*, 18.8.67
[9] Hilary Spurling, *Spectator*, 26.8.67
[10] Hilary Spurling, ibid.
[11] P. Toomey, op. cit.
[12] J.W. Lambert *Sunday Times*, 20.8.67
[13] Milton Shulman, op. cit.

Some felt that the production flagged over its three hours. The dialogue is not tight, witty repartee, but tends to spread itself out. The direction, however, was very intelligent.

> *'With this production Trevor Nunn establishes himself in the front row of young directors … His opening scene between Loveless and Amanda is idyllic, almost Chekhov in mood. In the dim evening light she sits on a garden swing, making desultory conversation. In the nature of events, her husband, whom she loves, will be unfaithful to her – not because he doesn't love her, but because he's – well, a man. The scene is full of the anticipation of regret.'*[14]

The production was colour-coded. 'Anything to do with pride or vanity is pink, anything to do with sophistication one suggests by grey or silver and the romantics are in rice-blue'[15] When the girls get the men out of the way they 'drop their fine manners and bring out drinks and clay pipes'.[16] Donald Sinden, revelling in the egregious Lord Foppington, appeared with fairy lights in his wig and a little Father Christmas. 'You may keep the fairy lights,' Trevor Nunn's note read, 'but cut the Father Christmas'.

'Oh yes, Trevor,' Susan told her director, when asked if she knew how she was going to play Amanda, 'like a fish swimming backwards'.[17] Nobody knew what she meant, but it seemed to make her happy. Tim Wylton played Lory, Young Fashion's servant. He writes that the RSC then:

> *'…wasn't pompous or over-intellectual; it was FUN. I wonder sometimes if it is still like that. Susan was part of that fun … She was, of course, stunning to look at and appeared to have no physical inhibitions. She moved like an untamed gazelle. The awful phrase that comes to mind is 'she was so alive'. I once gave her a lift from London to Liverpool. She talked non-stop all the way. It drove me mad. And now I look back with nostalgia and great*

---

[14] Frank Marcus, *Plays and Players*, Oct. 1967
[15] Michael Billington, *The Times*, 15.8.67
[16] Irving Wardle *The Times*, 18.8.67
[17] Norman Rodway, interview 18.2.98

*affection. In my humble opinion – as an actress she never lied … [she]
became one of our finest actresses'.*[18]

Susan made a deep impression on Frances de la Tour (Hoyden) and Lila Kaye.
Frances thought the production wonderful, but not quite Susan's 'moment'.
Nevertheless…

*'I thought she was brilliant, literally; she had a brilliant aura around her and
could be, when asked to be, brilliantly funny. When I first met her I envied
her silence, her long hair, her determined ambition and her purple plastic
handbag! (made by her designer sister). I wanted to be like her. Some time
later I realised she was just being herself, and I discovered I had acquired,
perhaps via her, a similar stubbornness. I was in Brook's* A Midsummer
Night's Dream *at the time. I felt it in* Duet for One *and* Moon for the
Misbegotten *and in many other productions I had been in.*

*Of all the actresses of my generation that I know, I think of her being the one
who could so easily have brought her magic to those parts I did. Sometimes
we get very possessive about the parts we play but she made me feel that they
should be shared (even if they weren't). And it isn't just because she died that
I admit this, but … I was deeply, deeply shocked and saddened at her
passing, and am still. She was beautiful and talented and full of life, and if
nothing else (although there was plenty else) I remember her wicked sense of
humour and outrageously funny laugh.'* [19]

It is fascinating to think of Frances as an alter ego to Susan. Peter Barkworth
compared them for vocal power. Frances followed Susan as Natalya in *The
Proposal*, but this was the only occasion on which they worked together. Both
were immensely tall and both had an enormous pent-up sensuality. Frances
deployed this quality with great comic effect here as Hoyden, hungry for a
husband, and of course, most famously, as Miss Jones in *Rising Damp*. If Susan
had ever had a TV showcase of that quality, she would surely have acquired a
well-deserved reputation as a comedienne.

---

[18] Tim Wylton, letter to author 11.11.97
[19] Frances de la Tour, letter to author 28.10.97

Susan struck up a cheery relationship with Lila Kaye, who played the nurse. She was to call her 'Smelly Boots' Kaye, because of the cramped condition of the changing room. Lila was always to use the name when phoning Sue.

The next play was *The Criminals (Los Assasinos)* by the Cuban playwright Jose Triana, adapted by Adrian Mitchell. Two sisters, Beba (Susan) and Cuca (Brenda Bruce) play a series of games with their brother Lalo (Barrie Ingham). They are in a state of festering revolt:

> '*Do this. Do that. Do the other. I want my life. Every day of it, every hour, every minute. I want to do what I want to do. But my hands are chained up. My feet are chained up. There's a blindfold round my eyes. This house is my world. And this house is getting old, it's rotting away. Because of them. Them.*'[20]

They re-enact the stifling rituals of their daily life and fantasise about murdering their parents with knives. Cuca portrays the mother as stealing money to buy a dress and blaming the theft on Lalo, who is then beaten by his father. Lalo does not forgive. Elsewhere Cuca defends the parents against the other two, but the parents hate each other. Father thought marriage meant 'clothes, food, stability … a little company … and finally … a few little liberties (as if hitting himself internally) Idiot! … I never imagined what it would be like.'[21] The siblings fight, too, each trying in turn to break out of the rituals, but each being dragged back. At the end, they are about to recommence. It was all about a struggle for personal autonomy, according to Terry. The actors wore tracksuits to reduce naturalism.

It is a grim, grinding piece, like many a sixties play. The age found itself in a harsh director like Peter Brook and a craggy actress like Glenda Jackson. Much energy was spent in fierce destruction of old pieties and beliefs about the sanctity of family life. Manic laughter, mock-Gregorian chant and nursery rhymes are scattered through the dialogue here, with a kind of fee-fie-fo-fum quality of threat; they are juveniles in revolt. It was generally execrated. B.A. Young thought that the 'operatic scale of emotion' was a result of Terry Hands forcing things

---

[20] Jose Triana, *Los Assasinos*, translated and adapted Adrian Mitchell, 1:11 (cue copy, RSC archive)
[21] Op. cit. II: 25

'unmercifully, far beyond what Miss Fleetwood or Mr Ingham is capable of and only just coming within the broad range of Miss Bruce.' [22]

The cause of Cuban culture was in the air, and some of the reactions were political. The *Morning Star* said it was a 'powerful and eloquent play for our time', while the *Daily Sketch* called it 'the dullest play that has ever been'. 'Less in it than meets the eye,' wrote W.A. Darlington.[23] Some audiences began to barrack even before the interval. 'The gallery, patient for many months now, mutinied noisily last night. Taking their cue from a line 'What should I do with this knife?' they came back fast with 'Stick it in the author!'[24] Peter Hall liked it, however, and so Terry survived.

And Susan? She loved it. 'We were on stage practically the whole time. I loved it – wild and wonderful, though I nearly lost my thumb at one performance. There were two enormous kitchen knives that had to be fairly sharp, as I had to cut a piece of cloth – that particular night I had a temperature of 103, but couldn't *not* go on – it would have been pretty difficult for an understudy – and the stage manager had taken the knives to be sharpened by a professional sharpener and they were like razors … I didn't feel any pain at all on stage, I suppose it was the adrenalin. I still have the scars'.[25] She winked at the others to assure them that she was ok. She always relished horror; it was part of her appetite for life. She was singled out for praise, as:

'*a new recruit to the company of immense interest and promise*'.

'*Susan Fleetwood is a new name to me and I shall remember her in* The Criminals *for giving the play everything she has got, especially when called upon to imitate the character's father and father's friends.*'

---

[22] B.A. Young, *Financial Times*, 29.9.67
[23] Jack Sutherland, *Morning Star*, 30.9.67, Fergus Cashin, *Daily Sketch* 29.9.67, W.A. Darlington, *Daily Telegraph* 29.9.67
[24] Felix Barker, *Evening News*, 29.9.67
[25] P. Toomey, op. cit.

'Miss Fleetwood shows what an exceedingly varied actress she can be. Her
time will come again, though in the next play she may not have to
impersonate a typewriter with a couple of knives.' [26]

Susan showed a sinister and destructive energy here, as she did later in Westphal's
'monkey' play of 1972.

In May 1968 *Under Milk Wood* was revived, with Sheila Allen and Susan
covering all the female parts. J.C. Trewin thought that they 'could hardly be
treated with more directness and enjoyment'.[27] Peter Gordon, in the cast, recalls
Susan's 'vinegary' quality as Mrs Ogmore Pritchard, 'and to this day I can hear
Mrs Pugh saying to her unfortunate tea-bringing husband in rasping sour tones
'Too much milk! ... Too much sugar then!' ... On the other hand, I remember
the mischievous virginal warmth of Gossamer Beynor's – 'I'll sin till I blow up!'[28]

In 1968-9 there were two parts she did not enjoy. One was Isabella, in Terry
Hands' *Women Beware Women*. She is betrothed, against her will, to Ward, a
'lewd half-wit'. 'Her grief and fear at the first meeting contrast strongly with the
composure with which – after she has learnt to serve her own pleasure with the
incestuous Hippolito – she submits, like a parcel of spoiled goods to the
bridegroom's inspection of her teeth'.[29] She initially rejects the advances of her
uncle, but when tricked (rather easily) into believing that he is not her uncle, she
accepts them willingly, while agreeing to marry the awful Ward, to deceive
society in general, and her father in particular. Susan was praised for her 'haughty
dignity', giving a 'taut study in suffering'.[30]

The part also calls for a secretive sexual gleefulness, and this the reviews don't
mention. Judi Dench played Bianca, the young wife who yields to the Duke's
vigorous seduction and then finds that she likes it. Judi had no great taste for the
play and some reviewers wondered why it had been revived. I cannot understand

---

[26] Helen Kretzmer, *Daily Sketch*, 29.9.67, Peter Roberts *Plays and Players* Dec. 1967, J.C. Trewin,
Birmingham Post, Sept. 29.9.67.
[27] J.C. Trewin , *Illustrated London News*, 11.3.68
[28] Peter Gordon, letter 13.12.97
[29] Hilary Spurling *Spectator,* 12.7.68
[30] S.B. *Stage and Television*, 10.7.68; Doreen Tanner *Liverpool Post*, 8.7.68.

why *not*. It is a more powerful piece than *The Changeling*, which is more frequently performed. It is an exact tragic counterpart to Ben Jonson's vision of a society quite happy with its own corruption, which it has reduced to a logical system. Middleton has a rare gift for transmitting sexual excitement. Anyway, the actors felt they needed comic relief from the sordor, provided offstage by Brewster Mason and Charles Thomas, the latter producing a rabbit at inopportune moments, like Tommy Cooper. Susan had as much a reputation as Judi for being a great giggler.

The other part was Regan, in Trevor Nunn's *King Lear* of 1968 (with Eric Porter as Lear). Judi Dench also hated this role, when she played it in 1976. 'Your goose is cooked the moment you come out'.[31] Regan must be Shakespeare's most vicious woman, all the more frightening when played by a pretty actress. Lear thinks her the next best daughter, after Cordelia:

'No, *Regan, thou shalt never have my curse.*
Thy tender-hefted nature shall not give
Thee o'er to harshness …'

Regan is the one who enjoys putting out Gloucester's eyes. 'One side will mock another. Th'other too!' She kills the servant who is trying to prevent it. Some reviewers thought Susan lightweight in the part; others thought she was accentuating Regan's youth, as 'a demure, giggling sadist who one can imagine as a spoiled child torturing her pets' and yet matching Sheila Allen's Goneril as 'beautifully vicious', making up a pair of 'sexy tigresses.'[32] Susan sprayed herself with water to give the effect of perspiring with lust for Edmund. Norman Rodway, as Edmund, thought this somewhat overdone. Shakespeare does leave a gap here. The girls' lust for Edmund is not portrayed from within. The dialogue to establish it is sparse and uninteresting, mere symbolic confirmation of Lear's view that destructive lust is the worst of all evils, destined to consume itself. Middleton would at least have allowed the lust to exist, verbally.

---

[31] Judi Dench, phone interview 16.11.98
[32] Irving Wardle, *The Times*, 11.4.68

'Lear depressed me', Susan said. 'I get terribly affected by the place I am in, and Lear was played in a grey box, and was very long, and nobody seemed very happy, anyway … I'm very affected by the parts I play. When I was doing Regan, I found that character was beginning to depress me after a time. I'd get very low. Then I'd rally and get on a real high. Never anywhere in between.' [33]

Other Shakespearean parts suited her somewhat better. In May 1968 she was Audrey in David Jones's *As You Like It*. 'Among the best of the newcomers is Susan Fleetwood as Audrey, gawkiest and freshest of simpletons'.[34] This was a general impression. Janet Suzman was Rosalind, having risen from Celia, in the previous year. She was on her way to her glorious Cleopatra of 1972. In October 1968 she scaled the intermediate height of Beatrice, in a Trevor Nunn *Much Ado*, in which Helen Mirren was Hero and Susan was Margaret. Susan was praised for wit and lightness of touch.

> *'Susan Fleetwood's Margaret – teasing Beatrice so indelicately and yet with*
> *an exquisite innate delicacy, or driving Hero frantic with the Duchess of*
> *Milan's gorgeous gown – is one of the most delectable things in this*
> *production'.*[35]

Susan's appearance as Cassandra in John Barton's *Troilus and Cressida* of 1968 was necessarily brief, but it registered. 'Susan Fleetwood, in the brief outcries of Cassandra, proves again what a commanding young actress she is.'[36]

> *'Susan Fleetwood, as the mad prophetess Cassandra, swoops on to the stage*
> *like a dragonfly'.*[37] *Hilary Spurling thought she suggested 'a hell of pain'.*[38]

Helen Mirren was Cressida, Michael Williams, Troilus, Norman Rodway, Thersites, and Alan Howard, Achilles.

---

[33] P. Toomey, op. cit.
[34] J.C. Trewin, *Birmingham Evening Post*, 22.5.68
[35] Hilary Spurling, *Spectator*, 25.10.68
[36] J.C. Trewin, *Illustrated London News*, 17.8.68
[37] W.T., *Nottingham Evening Post*, 9.8.68
[38] Hilary Spurling, *Spectator*, 16.8.68

Two Gentlemen of Verona is a more pallid play than any of these, but Gareth Morgan's production of 1969 gave Susan a chance to shine as Julia. The reviews were exceptionally welcoming.

> 'Susan Fleetwood as Julia patently enjoys her first opportunity as an RSC member to reveal her talent for comedy'.[39]

> 'Susan Fleetwood for the first time has an opportunity with the RSC to show what a poignantly witty actress she can be. Her Julia is sparklingly graceful; there are moments when she alone, by the simplicity of her acting, seems to bridge with just a moment of revelation the gap between chastity and romance.'[40]

> 'Susan Fleetwood presents a pretty and graceful picture of a young girl who simpers and giggles and is wholly in love with the beauty and surprise that life holds in store for her.'[41]

> 'Young, innocent and excitable, she matures overnight when, disguised as Celia, she witnesses Proteus's deceit.'[42]

These observations, especially the last one concerning sudden maturity, make us wonder how she would have been as Juliet. Terry Hands had a plan to have her play opposite David Warner as Romeo, to have two tall, commanding people in the roles, but alas, it never came to pass.

Pericles is not often staged. Some other hand than Shakespeare's, and a very clumsy one, is much evident, especially over the first two acts. It is an archaic, episodic story, out of which emerges a strange romance. In his 1969 production, Terry Hands was to triumph over this difficult material, in a great achievement both for himself and Susan, who played both mother and daughter, Thaisa and Marina.

---

[39] N.B.W., *Birmingham Mail*, 4.9.69
[40] G. Morgan, *Birmingham Post*, 4.9.69
[41] Richard Yates, *Leamington Spa Courier*, 12.9.69
[42] *Stage and Televsion Today*, 4.9.69

'I loved it,' Susan said. 'Visually it was so exciting. I really wanted to go out and see it. That season was a very happy experience.'[43] Terry Hands believes that all the Shakespeare texts, as we have them, are compilations, so it is the director's job to make sense of them. Costumes and sets were kept very simple for this, and a proper, thoughtful restraint was felt in the acting of both Susan and Ian Richardson, as Pericles. King Pericles abandons the body of his wife, Thaisa, in a storm at sea, and leaves his daughter, Marina, born on the same voyage, to be brought up by a royal couple he trusts. Thaisa is rescued and brought back from death's door by a skilled physician; she goes to live in the temple of Diana. Marina is about to be murdered by the queen left in charge of her, envious that her own daughter is eclipsed by Marina's virtues.

> 'Poor maid,
> Born in a tempest when my mother died,
> This world to me is as a lasting storm,
> Whirring me from my friends.'

Pirates suddenly appear and abduct Marina. They sell her to a brothel keeper, but she is so supremely and confidently virtuous that she seems set to ruin the business, by awakening a conscience in all the clients, and reducing them to a comic level of incompetence.

> 'She has here spoken holy words to the Lord Lysimachus.
> – O, abominable!
> She makes our profession as it were stink afore the face of the gods.
> – Marry, hang her up for ever!
> We must either get her ravished or be rid of her…'

Pericles comes to where she lives and she is held capable of bringing him out of the catatonic melancholy to which he has succumbed. He recognises her and is distracted by joy. He speaks of the music of the spheres 'that only she and I could hear' writes Ian Richardson, 'and we would hum it together very quietly. I think

---

[43] P. Toomey op. cit.

that this was her idea'.[44] Diana, goddess of chastity, then tells him in a dream to go to Ephesus, to be happy; there he meets Thaisa. Susan was convinced that Shakespeare meant mother and daughter to be two sides of one coin. 'It is only when she has suffered as Marina that they can know one another spiritually. Pericles, too, suffers and becomes ripe spiritually. Thaisa represents the physical side, Marina the spiritual' … both are 'much more like me than the parts I have played previously, such as Lady Macbeth. Previously I have been technically accomplished without being personally involved'.[45] At the end, another actress, Susan Sheers, stands in for Marina, as Susan reverts to Thaisa. For John Broome, the choreographer, this was the high point. '…the love-duet between Pericles and Thaisa. This was performed in silence: two slowly moving, near naked bodies in a series of gently changing statuesque relationships. Both were superb, and I can only describe Susan's action as effortless sculptural flow. I have stressed effortless again, and this was indeed the hallmark of her bearing. Few actresses have this ease and restraint to such a high degree.'[46]

Reviewers judged her 'superbly graceful', 'exquisitely carved in her double role'. She 'flashes her dark eyes and with poise and beauty steals the hearts of the audience with action befitting both her roles … miraculously, she retains her dignity even when threatened with being impaled on a priapic totem … Miss Fleetwood … dressed in a … flowing veil, still somehow suggests the marble limbs and fluttering drapery of a Renaissance painting.'[47] Juliet Aykroyd (Antiocus' daughter) thought that J.C. Trewin had the best phrase for Susan's acting – 'healing simplicity'.[48] Susan thought that it was a 'play of pure emotion … at rehearsals you could watch the audience weeping, they were so moved'.[49] It was group emotion, Benedict Nightingale thought, an exalted feeling of ritual successfully performed, somewhat like the last scene of *The Winter's Tale*. There is no dramatic struggle with villainy, which is destroyed off-stage. Plato and Yeats

---

[44] Ian Richardson, letter to author, 21.5.99
[45] Susan interviewed by Laura Gillan, *Wolverhampton Express and Star*, 2.4.69
[46] John Broome, letter to author, 3.1.99
[47] W.T. *Nottingham Evening Post*, 3.4.69, M.K, *Worcester Evening News*, 3.4.69, Francis Martin, *Sunday Telegraph*, 6.4.69, H. Spurling, *Spectator* 11.4.69.
[48] J.C. Trewin, *Illustrated London News*, 19.4.69
[49] Laura Gillan, op. cit.

were mentioned to suggest the production's poetic unity. There were no dissenting voices in the chorus of praise.

Susan's two acting triumphs of this period, then, were Amanda and Marina: two studies in chastity. The chance to be openly aggressive and sexually sly had not appealed to her. Actresses do not commonly shine for their portrayals of chastity. When they first appeared on the stage in the Restoration period the puritans accused them, with some justification, of being whores hawking their wares. With no hint of priggishness, however, and with much human warmth and comedy, Susan had drawn that quality out of some depth in herself, and made it live on the stage. It came out as an innate gift, like a clarity of vision that takes one towards what one truly wants. It only has significance, of course, as the gift of a supremely beautiful young woman.

Had Terry had his way, all the ladies would have gone bare-breasted, but they refused. Susan did wear a very thin and revealing tunic. Ian Richardson recalls her tweaking her nipples to get them up before going on stage. She was not one to hide her light under a bushel. Charles Dance thought she had 'the best legs in the business' and in this age of the miniskirt she took full advantage to show them off. Nowadays the Perennially Indignant flare up at the mention of such things being among the assets of an actress, but to hell with them.

In 1973 Susan reacted to the suggestion that she was pretty:

'Oh, for heaven's sake! I never think of myself at all like that. I think of myself as a rather hard-working, tall, serious idiot. I have a very odd face.' [50]

She was perhaps thinking of being labelled stereotypically pretty, but I still side with Stanley Kowalski, who 'never met a woman that didn't know if she was good-looking or not.'

The photographs included in this book show a woman of very different sorts of beauty at various stages of her life, but all are equally striking.

---

[50] Ian Woodward, 'Stars Ascending', 1973, periodical unidentified.

IV.   The Cambridge Theatre Company and the RSC again

In 1970 Susan took a break from the RSC.

'When I am working with mates continuously, for a very long time, if I do something outrageous, if I try something new, people are inclined to say, 'It's Sue, doing her thing', and that I find inhibiting. Working with new people can give you a new lease of life.' [1]

There was one blind alley in the year, the chance to play opposite John Hurt in a film called *Mr Forbush and the Penguins*; the offer was withdrawn and she was replaced by Hayley Mills. Susan was good and mad about it. It turned out to be not much of a part, however. Hayley sits about looking pretty waiting for John Hurt (Forbush) to mature from being a rich, fashionable boy by looking after his penguins in the Arctic. The penguins are the best thing in the film. When Susan saw it, resentment faded. 'It's a tough world,' she said when asked about it a year later, 'but I am very, very busy.' [2]

So she was. She had joined Richard Cottrell's Cambridge Theatre Company. This had been founded in 1969 as an offshoot of the Prospect Company, a touring company launched in 1960, based on the Old Vic. Originally, Prospect was to have four months at the Old Vic, to be followed by English Opera and Ballet Rambert, while they were on tour. This was an attempted revival of Lilian Baylis's dream of major art companies all working harmoniously together, but the politics proved too complex. The simplified outcome for drama was that Prospect would tour with classical pieces, while the Cambridge company would put on modern plays. They were based in the Arts Theatre, Cambridge, and funded by Cambridge Council, the Arts Theatre Trust, and the Arts Council. Lila Kedrova

---

[1] Philippa Toomey, 'Work as Therapy', *Times Saturday Review*, 21.12.74
[2] Scottish Sunday Express, 18.4.71

and Ian McKellan came along in the first year. Russian-born Lila, dubbed 'one of the world's great actresses' [3] by the *Guardian*, came with a huge reputation from the Paris stage, and her Oscar from *Zorba the Greek*. She won the *Evening Standard* award for actress of the year. Vivian Leigh had refused to come to Cottrell's *Cherry Orchard* in 1967, so he was asked, by Toby Robertson, who in all the world he'd like for Ranyevskaia. He said 'Lila Kedrova' and was surprised to get her. McKellan had soared to stardom at the Edinburgh Festival in 1969, with his portrayals of Richard II and Edward II. It says much for Richard Cottrell (who had directed the *Richard II*) that such actors were ready to work under him for modest pay and the rigours of touring.

The first play was *The Seagull*, with Lila as Irina Arkadina and Susan as Nina. It opened at the Arts Theatre, Cambridge, on July 21ˢᵗ 1970. Lila arrived in a state, having left her jewel box on the train. 'They were given to my father by the Czar!' She couldn't act without them, so it was just as well that they were found at Kings Lynn, and returned. She and Susan got on fine. Cottrell was as sure of Susan as he was of Lila. She had come to audition at his flat in Charlotte Street, dressed all in white. He broke his usual habit by giving her the part immediately on hearing her read.[4] 'My happiest times have been in Chekhov – most actors will tell you that,' she said in 1974.[5]

In the nineties, she said: 'There was a lot of Nina in me twenty years ago'.[6] She agreed with Richard Cottrell that Nina's life was about the sacrifice necessary for a life dedicated to art; and that she probably would turn out to be a good actress, it's just that this cost her a great deal. The blind hero-worship that is one of Nina's great weaknesses was definitely not one of Susan's. Don Chapman wrote that the production was not melancholy and elegiac, but full of strong, colourful, well-projected emotion. 'Susan Fleetwood pulses with the impulsive naive zeal for life of Nina.'[7] The Cambridge reviewer said that 'Chekhov can seldom have seemed so light-hearted. Even at moments of the deepest tragedy, the characters'

---

[3] *Guardian*, 30.10.70
[4] Richard Cottrell, interview 11.8.99
[5] 'Work as Therapy' op. cit.
[6] Vera Lustig, *Plays and Players*, February 1991
[7] Don Chapman, *Oxford Mail*, 18.4.70

realisation of it is often amusing because of their nervous change of mood. Miss Fleetwood moves between the girl's early naive wonder at the man's worldliness and gentle resignation to a hopeless acceptance that, although he has cast her to one side, she cannot live wholly without him. Nina's first meeting with Trepliov is also most moving, for the girl is so tragically a pathetic little animal fallen prey to an inevitable fate.'[8] It moved on to the Yvonne Arnaud Theatre, Guildford, and the New Theatre, Oxford (now the Apollo). In a near-ecstatic review, the Yvonne Arnaud critic said:

> 'The Nina is superb. Despite a rather too robust appearance, Susan Fleetwood personifies the corruption of innocence with a shining integrity and grace that move one to tears. In her scenes with Trigorin her worship of the great writer is beautifully stated, and in the final scene with Konstantin they earn a tribute of total silence.'[9]

The next piece was George Farquhar's *The Recruiting Officer*, a late Restoration comedy of 1706. The company took it from the Ashcroft theatre, Croydon, to the Arts, Cambridge, the Theatre Royal, Brighton, the Grand Theatre, Leeds, the Grand Theatre, Swansea, and the Nuffield, Southampton, from October to November 1970. Susan played Sylvia, an attractive girl who turns out to be an heiress too. It is said of her that 'there's something in that girl more than Woman, her Sex is but a foil to her'.[10] Her friend Melinda says, more bluntly, 'you have the constitution of a horse!'[11]

She is obviously a fit partner for Captain Plume (Ian McKellan), the brains behind the unscrupulous recruiting drive. He is equally amoral in his pursuit of Rose, an innocent country girl who sells chickens; this leads to much saucy innuendo. Sylvia returns disguised as Wilful, another captain, which part she says she is sure to carry off well with enough swagger, since that's all there is to it. She gets Rose away from Plume and beds her. Rose may not be quite sure of what to expect, but certainly it was more. Her brother Bullock has Wilful arrested, but

---

[8] Deryck Hayes, *Cambridgey Evening News*, 22.7.70
[9] J.W.P. *Surrey Advertiser and County Times*, 7.8.70
[10] *The Recruiting Officer*, Act I, scene i lines 252-4
[11] Act I, scene ii, lines 128-9

figures out eventually who he/she is. 'I altered my Outside, because I am the same within, and only laid by the Woman to make sure of my Man.' [12] It's not quite clear how Plume has been tested and found true, but apparently he has.

The Cambridge critic said that they fully realised a delicate moment on stage when they discovered the magnetism that was drawing them towards each other. Plume resolves to 'raise Recruits the Matrimonial Way'. [13] With her height and her deep voice Susan was a natural for the pretend- male part, which of course often served her turn in Shakespeare. She cut a 'delectable figure' that wasn't exactly convincing, but worked very well in the context. [14]

In this vein of 'more than a woman', she played Lady Rodolpha Lumbercourt in a little-known play, Charles Macklin's *Man of the World*, a comedy of 1781, revived for 1971. She is hauled in by her elders to marry the hapless hero, Egerton, who finds her pretty formidable; 'her spirits are inexhaustible; her parts strong and lively, with a sagacity that discerns, and a talent not unhappy in pointing out the weak side of whatever comes before her'.[15] She is noisy, improper, and provincial;

> *Why, yeer orfleats, capillares, lemonades, and ow yeer slips-slops, wi which ye drench yeer wembs, when ye are dancing – upon honour, they always make a swish- swash in my bowels, and gi' me the wooly-wambles.*
>
> *Omnes: Ha, ha, ha.*
>
> *Lord Lumbercourt: Ho, ho, ho! you indelicate creature …*[16]

Egerton is right to think her clever behind this colourful facade. Although she demands to be wooed in 'amorous phrenzy', and weeps to be rejected, she cheers up quickly on hearing that Egerton loves Another, for she does too – his brother. She packs off to marry him at the end of the play. This sort of broad comedy is not normally associated with Susan, but there it is.

---

[12] Act V, scene vi, lines 153-6
[13] Act V, sc.v, line 220
[14] *Croydon Advertiser*, 9.10.70
[15] *Four Comedies by Charles Macklin*, ed. J.O.Bartily, Sidgwick and Jackson 1968. Act I, p.207
[16] op. cit. Act II, p.229

'Susan Fleetwood's boisterous Lady Rodolpha Lumbercourt, with a Scots accent, a romantic secret and a nice line in deliberate faux pas *is an irresistible piece of comic invention'.*[17]

'Red-lipped, beaming and loudly Scottish, Susan Fleetwood detonates the surrounding genteel atmosphere with a series of radiantly awful social gaffes, laying about her with a silk scarf, flinging herself on her father's lap, and going down on all fours to the bowing Sir Pertinax ... high comedy from out of the overflow of good spirits[18] *... a cross between a deb and a Dalmatian.'*[19]

It is remarkable that this ran in tandem with *Hamlet* just after that was launched in the spring of 1971. Susan had been drawn to play Ophelia because of that real contact the reviewer had noticed with McKellan, whom Harold Hobson was now calling 'the greatest Shakespearean actor alive'. Susan and Ian were both excellent company members. When they all got out to Rome, Ian knew all the right people, such as Antonioni's nephew, so they had entrees to sophisticated parties. Susan and Nickolas Grace gazed on in awe. Ian and she were close friends for a while. 'Yah! You only have me around to advertise your heterosexuality', she would say, sticking her head out of the window of his mews flat to make sure that the neighbours noticed her presence.

This Prospect production went to the Edinburgh Festival in 1971. After appearing at the Wolverhampton Grand, it went on to the Nottingham Playhouse, Aberdeen, Edinburgh, Glasgow, Cardiff and Brighton, before a European tour began, involving Belgium, Holland, Germany, Austria, Switzerland and Italy. The Greek shipping tycoon and theatrical impresario Sir Eddie Kulukundis – a truly Homeric person, of profound good humour and curly grey beard – saw it in the Hague, and invited the whole cast to a midnight feast at his hotel, to discuss its future.

McKellan and his chosen director Robert Chetwyn, wanted it put on in the West End and then filmed. Sir Eddie duly arranged this. It appeared at the Cambridge

---

[17] John Barber, *Daily Telegraph* 6.8.71
[18] Irving Wardle, *The Times*, 12.4.71
[19] B.A. Young, *Financial Times* 17.4.71

Theatre, London, in August, and was screened by BBC2 on September 23rd 1972. This is one of the first pieces of Susan's work to be preserved on tape, and it is a huge relief to be able to match one's own impressions against those of reviewers. Sir Eddie thought that David Giles made a superb job of putting the production onto the TV screen. Robert Chetwyn has one reservation, that the sepia tones of the stage could not be transferred. They had cast a poetic and internal tone over Hamlet's soliloquies. (When the cast discussed what to do with 'To be or not to be', McKellan had a rather original suggestion; cut it. It stayed, of course.) Sir Eddie got them to restore another proposed cut, the line 'Rosencrantz and Guildenstern are dead', as Tom Stoppard's play of that name was popular then, and he thought it would spark something in a young audience. It was a production for young people.[20] Now-familiar actors were in a youthful, glamorous phase. McKellan and Julian Curry (the latter as Horatio) have splendid hair, and Tim Piggott-Smith (as Laertes), although austerely cropped, is very fresh of face. The direction wasn't masterful. 'Darlings, we've just got to make up our own minds', Susan told the others. She had decided how to be Ophelia. She rejected the offer of a small bra, on the grounds that the original girl wouldn't have worn one.

One problem in playing Ophelia, 'the young, the beautiful, the harmless and the pious' is to guess how to pitch the relationship with Hamlet at the beginning. Shakespeare has left a gap here, for how can we imagine such a girl satisfying more than a portion of Hamlet's extraordinary personality? Hamlet perhaps follows his father in choosing a lady too small for his capacious mind, and ambition. We never, of course, see the relationship before Polonius, and then the king, start interfering with it. The Branagh film was clear that they had enjoyed sexual relations, and I have seen many a playful Ophelia, who enjoyed coquetting with her brother, let alone Hamlet. Not Susan. She was a deadly serious Ophelia, so much so that one could not imagine what she would have been like in an ordinary, daily context.

---

[20] Sir Eddie Kulukundris, OBE, interview 18.5.99

When we first see her she is demolishing a flower, and she continues to do this faster when she hears Hamlet abused. She clutches Laertes' hand and traces a pattern upon it while he is talking. He tries a little humour, to no effect. She closes her eyes in pain after hearing Polonius' instructions to break off with Hamlet. When Hamlet rails at her, he is himself near-hysterical, in a tormented world of his own, and so there cannot be any chemistry between them. She spins round in grief before delivering the speech 'O, what a noble mind is here o'erthrown …' She is made nervous by the players throwing costumes and carpets about. In the play-scene, Claudius decides to make a joke of Hamlet's talking of Polonius as 'so capital a calf'. The court laughs, but not Ophelia. Her line to Hamlet 'You are merry, my lord' is given with a brief sense of relief; she really did not understand his bitter, sexual jokes.

Susan worked very hard on the mad scenes. She comes in clacking a wooden crucifix. Neither a cold Claudius (John Woodvine) nor an alcoholic Gertrude (Faith Brook), clutching her goblet, want to hear her. She sings beautifully, but breaks off into a tiny scream at the end of;

> *He is dead and gone,*
> *At his head a grass-green turf,*
> *At his heels a stone …*

and bursts into tears at the end of the bawdy song 'By Cock, they are to blame'. Her way of crying is truly harrowing to watch. Her whole face is contorted, and her wide mouth sags like a battered old satchel. When Laertes is on stage she lectures him as a child might, and then sits giving flowers to Gertrude, putting some into her hair. Gertrude laughs, vaguely and inanely, and staggers out utterly bewildered at the end of the scene. (Why does she drink? Is it because of how much she knows, or suspects? The director successfully made these eternal questions hang all the more ominously in the air.) The two women have been unable to forge a bond, and both remain desperately lonely.

> *'I had not known so heart-breaking an Ophelia.'* [21]

---

[21] J.C. Trewin, *Illustrated London News* Oct. 1971

'...touchingly human...' [22]

'a supreme and superb Ophelia, an outworn girl who goes down in a crazed, blank apprehension of lovelessness." [23]

Some of the praise was qualified by a perception of a certain sexual power in her that had gone awry – ' an overgrown child', ' a repressed, awkward virgin, primly gawky', someone with 'disturbing signs of sexual mania', a 'statuesque' Ophelia (who) 'could have been Hamlet's nurse'. [24]

These are odd comments. What exactly is 'sexual mania'? And must Ophelia always look frail and diminutive? She found the part a strain. 'I get very affected by the parts I play, and I became a bit miserable, being smashed every night. It made me very aggressive during the day, because I was having to suppress all that feeling in the evening. Ophelia is always hit against. She never makes the move.' [25]

On July 27th she came down with an ulcerated throat, but carried straight on. When they were busy making the tape, she told Richard Cottrell that McKellan's ego had taken a beating from the number of bad reviews. 'What daft buggers we all are,' she mused, [26] 'to go to all the trouble.'

The perception that there was a certain throttled-back power in Susan's acting was real. In the same year as this, she made her first venture into television, with a play based on A.E. Coppard's story *The Watercress Girl*. This went out on Granada on September 16th, and is preserved on tape. She plays Mary McDowell, young and attractive in a sleepy-eyed, sensual way. We first see her bending over in water, cutting watercress, with her skirts tucked dangerously high. Frank Oppidan, a straight, hard-working craftsman, woos her, but she refuses to wed him, although their sexual relations are unrestrained.

[22] John Peter, *Sunday Times* 16.5.71
[23] Nicholas de Jongh, *Guardian* 6.8.71
[24] R.Bryden, *Observer Review* 18.4.71, Milton Shulman, *Evening Standard* 6.8.71; Frank Marcus, *Sunday Telegraph* 15.8.71; Irving Wardle, *Times* 16.4.71
[25] *Plays and Players* June 1973
[26] R. Cottrell interview 11.8.99

Gareth Thomas (as Frank) recalls with regret that Susan kept her knickers on during the love scenes. (Sometimes a mere strip of cloth suffices; Terry Southern's novel *Blue Movie* will intrigue the curious on these matters.) 'I'll go with you! But I'll not wed you. Nor no man,' she cries, in a harsh, determined voice. It is a very odd moral choice for a girl of those Thomas Hardy times. He leaves her, and she writes, but in such a veiled fashion that he never guesses that she is with child. It is delivered, dead. Frank is by then courting a respectable, middle-class girl, Elizabeth Planteney. Mary throws vitriol in her face, which ruins her chances of every marrying, it is understood. Mary gets eighteen months for this, reduced to twelve. Frank threatens to throw vitriol on her, to get a proper revenge for Elizabeth, but it is clear he cannot go through with it. Mary explains that she wouldn't marry because it would have revealed her father's illegitimacy. She expected Frank to come and see how she was when she wrote.

Frank has a great gift for feeling sorry for himself, saying that he never knew he had a son coming, or existent, or gone, as he is now. 'So I'm just nothing'. He will start up again with Mary. Although she orders him away, her sleepy, sexually powerful look is still on him, undiminished by what she has been through. It is the wholly unassuming and gentle Elizabeth who is the loser. Susan has a dangerous look throughout, not at all sly, but that of a girl who does not know herself or what she is capable of: passionately jealous and demanding, but also giving and reliable. Gareth and Susan almost had an affair, but they were both committed to other people at the time, so nothing happened. On a train journey together, they wept over it.[27]

In 1972 she was also in a curious *piece noire*. Prospect put on Richard Cottrell's translation of a French play by Eric Westphal called *You and Your Clouds*, known in some quarters as 'the Monkey play'. It had won a prize in France from a panel that included Ionesco. Susan played the deeply disturbed Ermentine, a recluse who is 'not herself' when her clouds come, 'her delicate beauty ... only emphasising the tragedy of the girl's derangement.'[28] She practises vivisection on monkeys secretly, and when a young brush salesman turns up, she lures him into

---

[27] Gareth Thomas, phone interview 13.8.99
[28] G.M.P. *Croydon Advertiser* 28.1.72

the back room and chains him up. She has a sister, Adele (played by Rene Asherson), a solemn believer in a better, science-based future. The scene ends when Adele appears, looks into the room and says 'no!' One assumes the worst, but in the next scene he is alive and well; once released, he threatens them with the law. Ermentine says she'll lie, Adele will support her, and it will all be like a Racine play (*Phedre*, presumably). He accepts 700 francs as compensation. In the next scene Ermentine triumphs over a chained-up Adele, who is on the point of death (shades of *Whatever Happened to Baby Jane?*). Ermentine hates her for her perfections, although she agrees that she cannot survive without her. Adele dies unresistingly.

What does one make of this? On the one hand, Adele seems naive and defenceless in her idealism and acceptance of the perversion of science practised by Ermentine; on the other, Ermentine passes into fantasy when she meets any opposition, confining her sadism to helpless animals. Perhaps it is a satire on the folly of not resisting, and covering up for a genuinely dangerous person. Cottrell chose it because there was a 'thundering good part' for Susan. She was to venture again into this territory, with Strindberg.

Susan returned to the RSC in 1972 to play in various historical pieces, among others. One, *Island of the Mighty*, by John Arden and Margaretta D'Arcy, was a disaster. It was a portrayal of post-Roman Britain, supposed to shed light on contemporary Ireland. Arden, however, thought that the production perverted the text, making the Romans noble and dignified, and the Celts into clowns. This only became clear to him late in rehearsals, and the cast voted not to follow his suggestion of changing the director, David Jones, at that stage. Arden and his wife, the co-author, thereupon picketed the theatre, and interrupted a performance. Emrys James, playing King Arthur, and hence with a certain authority, said they should put the matter to a vote by the audience, which again defeated John Arden. 'Right', he said 'we will never write for you again'. This carried some weight, as they shared a distinguished reputation, but it could not win them the day. His weeping wife dragged away some of the matting.[29]

---

[29] *Guardian* 27.11.72, 29.11.72; *Sunday Independent*, Dublin, 3.12.72; *Financial Times* 3.12.72

Controversy raged in the press. Trevor Nunn answered the charge that he and the company he led were dupes of the Establishment by pointing out the left-wing nature of much contemporary drama that they were putting on. This drew the wrath of Tory M.P. Angus Maude, who wanted to know why taxpayers' money was going on avowedly political works. Nunn replied that 'left-wing' was not capitalised, and that meant that it was a cultural drift rather than anything party-political. What strikes the modern reader or playgoer is how lucky Arden and his wife were to get their four-and-a-half hour play staged at all, with its small army of actors. Today it would not have a hope of seeing daylight. Tony Church, who played a Pictish poet, said that the cast could tell which bits had been written by Arden, and which, the inferior parts, by Margaretta D'Arcy, whom both he and Trevor Nunn blamed for the fracas.[30] 'I found it all unreadable. Susan, with her indifference to politics, thought it all a joke.' Her part, of a bondswoman, was very small. She is captive to various men, moralises a bit and gets killed early on. Very few actors were mentioned in the reviews; she not at all.

The Hollow Crown of 1973 was much more cheerful. John Barton directed this ensemble piece of 1961; it consists of recitations and performances of vignettes and anecdotes from history, from William I to Queen Victoria, and ending with the death of Arthur. Much fun came from the Scots accent of James I and the German-English of George III. Susan 'was particularly impressive for her performance as the fifteen year old 'historian' Jane Austen, and moralist and diarist Fanny Burney'.[31] In a piece of juvenilia, Jane Austen presented herself as partisan, prejudiced and ignorant, a devout Yorkist and supporter of Mary Queen of Scots. Ian Richardson, Tony Church and Donald Sinden appeared in it at different times. It was a perennially popular piece, and enjoyed an American tour.

In 1972 Susan appeared as the chorus leader in *Murder in the Cathedral*. The prestige of this play had somewhat faded since the late forties and fifties, when Peter Barkworth recalled actors thinking Eliot 'very good for diction', an offshoot of his general respectability. Eliot was, however, always Susan's favourite poet.

---

[30] Tony Church, phone interview 14.12.98
[31] J.H. *Solihull News* 21.7.72

Although this was the most successful of his plays, it is hard to feel that it is a piece of vibrant intensity. It is highly cerebral, with the careful mapping-out of the zones the characters inhabit, and the kaleidoscopic tricks of switching them about; Thomas Archbishop solves his problem of spiritual pride just by realising that he has it, and the sensual imagery of the chorus is used wholly negatively, on the page. Terry Hands hadn't changed his mind since staging the play in Everyman days. It was still to be ritualistic and impersonal, but now he wanted it infused with tremendous energy. The relation between Thomas and the chorus of women is sexual, and their guilt is purged in orgasmic fashion. Susan, as leader, 'accompanied the narrative of her vision of corruption by lying writhing on her back, thighs widely parted – facing *upstage* let me quickly reassure squeamish or voyeuristic readers. When she reaches an orgasmic climax ... in her exhaustion (she) is tenderly caressed by Beckett kneeling among the frightened women.'[32] Her vocal performance was equally well sustained. Her voice was described as 'beautiful but emotion-torn' and having 'an almost frightening intensity'.[33] She competes fiercely with a long drum-roll during the climactic speech 'I have smelt them, the death-bringers', where the acceptance of martyrdom *is* sexually expressed;

> 'I have consented, Lord Archbishop, have consented,
> Am torn away, subdued, violated,
> United to the spiritual flesh of nature,
> Mastered by the animal powers of spirit,
> Dominated by the lust of self-demolition,
> By the final uttermost death of spirit,
> By the final ecstasy of waste and shame ...'

This is more like a Dionysiac acceptance of destruction, with a strong embrace of horror, than any fit of shivering revulsion. Terry's direction was at its harshest and most demanding. 'Don't worry,' Susan told the cast, with a somewhat crooked smile, 'he's always like this.' He didn't hesitate to use details of their domestic life to illustrate what she shouldn't be doing. Several times she was on the point of

---

[32] J.W.Lambert *Sunday Times* 3.9.72
[33] D.A.C. *Coventry Evening Telegraph* 1.9.72; Valerie Grey *Evening Gazette* Colchester 1.9.72

tears, but never actually gave way. Sometimes the whole cast would be exhausted and tearful at the end of a performance. They would occasionally meet the cast of *Godspell*, playing nearby; they were having rather more fun.[34]

Was all the suffering worth it? Terry said he would take a recording of Sue to his desert island. Richard Pasco's Beckett was universally praised, but few reviewers took the play to their hearts and *Godspell* proved to be a distraction.

Between 1972 and 1974, a *Sturm und Drang* period for Susan, she played four major Shakespearean roles. There was some pain in working with Terry on *The Merchant of Venice*, where the lash was still on, but Portia gave her much more to hang on to, and the result was fine-spun romance. (It is pleasant to reflect on this side of Terry's work. His *Much Ado* of 1983, with Sinead Cusack and Derek Jacobi, was unforgettably tender and exalted.)

The main problem with the *Merchant* is the respective weight to give Shylock and Antonio. Unbridled sympathy for Shylock can overset the play and leave Act V wholly redundant. A good Portia is the right counterbalance to him. Susan rejoiced in Portia's strength:

> *'None of them, apart from Shylock, come anywhere near to Portia in strength ... Such an intelligent woman, and also passionate. Something I do find easy is to work on one big curve of emotion which can blanket a thought or intention. The problem is to stab that with intelligence. So playing her was a very good lesson for me. I'd feel a great emotional surge, but all the time I had to jolt myself into clear thinking, and train my mind to race ahead, because she goes at such a speed. She's always one step in front of everyone. Usually, of course, she is played by somebody older, but I think perhaps I shouldn't do Portia again later on – it works better for somebody young. There are reverberations of womanliness and boyishness there.'* [35]

If Portia is too confident of her position, her money and her husband, she could become haughty, and that would ruin the line 'Then must the Jew be merciful'

---

[34] Nickolas Grace, interview 24.8.99
[35] Gordon Gow, 'Shakespeare's Women', *Plays and Players* June 1973

in the trial scene. As a quick imperative, it is intolerable. One reviewer said that Susan showed a 'serenity of spirit' that made this line, and the famous speech on mercy 'a simple and unaffected appeal from reason to unreason'.[36] It was as though the thought had just occurred to her, as something beautiful and obvious. When Bassanio suggests abrogating the law, her lines;

> 'It must not be, there is no power in Venice
> Can alter a decree established ...'

were delivered under great pressure of grief. She didn't come to the scene with the answer ready; it came suddenly, in the middle, and of course just in time. When she gets the upper hand over Shylock she was 'adamant and menacing' ... 'a Portia who can match the Jew in venom and give him lessons in cruelty'.[37] I find that overstated, although I am only going on a sound recording. There is no venom in her use of the word 'Jew', which would be morally fatal to her cause, and there is a certain nervousness and vulnerability skipping through her words as she reins Shylock in. It all sounds beautifully judged.

According to Michael Billington, the modern way to see the play is as a real love-tussle between Portia and Antonio. Portia recognises how much hold Antonio has over Bassanio, and is frightened of it; she is torn several ways in the trial scene. This makes good sense of the otherwise tiresome ring-business of the fourth and fifth acts; something real is at stake. Bassanio does say;

> 'But life itself, my wife and all the world
> Are not with me esteem'd above thy life
> I would lose all, ay sacrifice them all
> Here to this devil, to deliver you ...'

Portia's retort, 'Your wife would give you little thanks for that / If she were by to hear you make the offer' got a good laugh, from its real thrust. Her earlier speech, after Bassanio has won her, beginning 'You see me, Lord Bassanio where I stand.'

---

[36] N.R. *Eastern Daily Press* 13.6.72
[37] John Barber, *Daily Telegraph*, 23.6.72

was described as 'brimming with enthusiasm. There is ecstasy in Miss Fleetwood's voice ... crystalline music to the ears'.[38]

> *'This house, these servants, and this same myself*
> *Are yours, my Lord, I give them with this ring ...'*

was cited as the height of her pleasure, but there is a pause before the second half of the second line, a rapid transition to a note of warning, rather like Juliet's 'If thou think'st I am too quickly won...' The touch of fear helps make her love real, like Juliet's. At the end, when she is about to reveal the triumph of her trickery, the line 'Speak not so grossly, you are all amazed', which can sound very prissy, was done with light mockery. She seemed to pronounce it as 'we are all amazed' in the recording, which sounds better. She is secure in her victory.

There is delightful comedy in the early part of the play, before she meets Bassanio. Morocco sounds like a good parody of Olivier's Othello. The actor handed Portia a cat as a present. Of all animals to work with on stage, cats must rank amongst the worst. Susan, not herself a cat person, was supposed to pick one from fourteen auditioning. One combined stage-fright and scene-stealing by escaping, and then interrupting monologues with his backstage yowlings.

Some reviews were fulsome in their praise.

> *'Susan Fleetwood is a star of the not-too-far-off future. Her Portia is supreme,*
> *coaxing and yet winsome ...*

> *'Susan Fleetwood is no fragile beauty hovering in the leafy glades of*
> *Belmont, but a buoyant lover.'*

> *'A wonderful Portia, too, from Susan Fleetwood, whose range from cool*
> *ladyship to tingling, yearning womanhood standing upon the edge of*
> *fulfillment is beautifully accomplished'.[39]*

> *'more openly and vulnerably in love with the unmeritable Bassanio than any*
> *Portia I've seen.'[40]*

---

[38] Jane Gowers, *Eastern Evening News* 13.6.72
[39] Philip Penfold, *Newcastle Evening Chronicle* 11.5.72; Allen Wright, *The Scotsman* 17.5.72; Jane Gowers, op. cit.

One was uncharacteristically critical, giving only the faint praise that Susan was 'well-spoken' and 'unaffected'.[41] Peter Lewis, Milton Shulman and Frank Marcus all disliked it.

In August 1973 she was the Princess of France in *Love's Labour's Lost* directed by David Jones with Ian Richardson as Berowne. Striking the right balance between levity and seriousness is essential with this play. 'Before anyone speaks a word, we see the four votaries taking up position to solemn music and casting their gay clothes into a coffin.'[42]

Catherine Itzin thought the director had caught a world of the young, ignorant of death. 'Susan Fleetwood's Princess is a really tough, intelligent, no-nonsense lady who gives the impression she knows she's playing for long-term life as well as short-term love.'

Benedict Nightingale found the production 'refreshingly unpretentious'. Some found it too slow and verbal, problems inherent in the text, and Michael Billington thought it all felt like high-school girls on an end of term spree. Susan was consistently well praised, 'a stylish ship's figurehead whose final supremacy is implicit throughout'; 'unstrained authority ... with a tone that catches the sunlight'; 'of the dozen enamoured suitors of the play, the only one to look really in love'; 'so much quiet authority that I was inclined to paraphrase Fortinbras – For she was likely ... to have been proved most royal.'[43]

When it came around again in February 1975, there were no hostile reviews at all. Michael Billington defined it as a play about the process of growing up, very evident in the Princess by the end. John Barber thought she 'guards from the beginning a strain of wistfulness, so that at the sad end she can respond convincingly as a woman of feeling.'[44]

---

[40] Benedict Nightingale, *New Statesman* 7.7.72
[41] Michael Billington, *Guardian* 23.6.72
[42] Irving Wardle, *Times* 2.8.73
[43] Cathy Itzen, *Plays and Players*, June 1973, Irving Wardle, *Times*, 8.8.73; J.C. Trewin, *Birmingham Post* 4.8.73; Michael Billington 8.8.73; John Barber, *Daily Telegraph* 8.8.73; Wendy Monck, *Stage and Television* 16.8.73
[44] John Barber, *Daily Telegraph* 2.5.75

Fellow actor Doyne Byrd thought her 'completely in her element... Looks, strength, charm, wit. Rising way above David Suchet and making Ian Richardson fight for his status. Waiting quiet and alone in the wings she was mesmerically beautiful.'[45]

In this second production, an old friend of hers, Norman Rodway, replaced Derek Smith as Holofernes. He developed a laugh suitable for the pedant, a high, staccato bark that Susan said reminded her of Basil Brush. He was for her, forever after, Basil Brush. Her sense of fun was fully alive. Doyne Byrd recalls her 'great humour, often ribald and robust. We had two Great Danes on Love's Labours, a different pair at each venue when touring America. Somewhere, I forget where, two huge beasts were being led off by Jan Labanowski having stolen the scene and Susan noticed the testicles of one. "Look at the size of those! Wait, wait! I want to feel the weight of them!" And she did, with a naughty-boy grin.' [46]

She had been offered the part of Rosaline, 'but she's the flash part, and since I knew I was going to play Kate I decided it would be a good idea to have someone else who was different, not a bravura person but a complicated and intense specimen. So I shall be delicate and tender and subtle with the Princess and razzamataz with Kate – hopefully.' [47] She was amazed to be offered this very different role, especially as there had been a *Taming of the Shrew* quite recently, with Janet Suzman as Kate, who had been, Susan said, 'so brilliant'. 'I don't see myself as her at all, but it's very much a play of chemistry and I'm not going into rehearsal with heavy ideas because I might miss out on something that will spark off between myself and Alan Bates, who's playing Petruchio.' [48]

In Clifford Williams' production, some reviewers thought that some of the energy of conflict between the lovers had been transferred to stage business. 'The chemistry between them is not right,' Michael Coveney wrote. Alan Bates' approach was 'offhand, casually materialistic.' [49] Some were surprised at her lack

---

[45] Doyne Byrd, letter to author 30.1.98
[46] Doyne Byrd, ibid
[47] Gordon Gow, op. cit.
[48] Gordon Gow, ibid.
[49] Michael Coveney, *Financial Times*, 21.9.73

of aggression. Michael Billington wrote that she 'goes down for the count quicker than a British heavyweight (she even allows Petruchio to massage her foot in the first encounter).'[50] 'This shrew is a dormouse,' another critic wrote.[51] The *Gloucester Citizen* reviewer came closest to Susan's own interpretation of the role:

'Susan Fleetwood gives a vigorous and accomplished performance, revealing a sympathetic, lonely and misunderstood character, who is noticeably attracted to Petruchio from the outset.'[52] Susan had said:

> '*I find Kate fascinating. She is an independent woman and although, outwardly, Petruchio spends the play taming her, he's far too intelligent to want to kill the very quality which makes her so attractive to him. Even in the last great speech when she talks of the obedience a wife owes to her husband, she is really saying that life with a man is equally giving and sharing, not submissive. It is interesting that in most of Shakespeare's plays it is the men who have to mature during the play by falling in love and at the end they are ready for partnership.*'[53]

Twenty-one years later in a radio discussion with Fiona Shaw and Paola Dionisotta, steered by Michael Billington, she recalled the part as though she had played it the day before, and she hadn't changed her mind in the least. She described Kate as a lively mind thwarted by her society, and hence driven to something they call madness. 'Her speech is cartoon and coarse, she has none of the linguistic resources of Beatrice. She likes meeting someone big enough to take on. The punters are excited at the revelation to the characters, there's a thunderbolt that happens when she meets him, and he with her. Why not choose something more interesting for the audience to watch – two characters that one hopes are going to bed together at the end of the play, and enjoy it, rather than ones that don't care about each other?' She does fight against the attraction at first, being 'violently defensive' and perhaps not understanding what is happening

---

[50] *Guardian* 26.9.73
[51] D.I. *Coventry Evening Telegraph*, 26.9.73
[52] L.S. *Gloucester Citizen*, 27.9.73
[53] Jane Evers, periodical undiscovered

to her. The treatment Petruchio metes out to her is in the interests of a final harmony. 'Because she's in an unbalanced state, she's clearly not a happy woman at the beginning of the story, and this is tough medicine he's gone for ... to break the code'.

They discuss her final speech of submission, with Billington suggesting that no modern actress could do it without irony. Paola Dionisotti said she had done it wholly that way, under Michael Bogdanov's direction, but had never felt she had grasped the part, and had made a pretty fair hash of it. Susan dissented from the idea. She had gone for 'utter simplicity; as little irony as possible'. (The reviews agree, and one said that the speech was received in 'puzzled silence'.)[54]

> 'The understanding was such that the journey they had had together during the play had resulted in a trust between them. Then when she made this offering of herself to him, it was an understanding that she would be receiving the same from him. It was rather a holy, rather a simple, rather solemn, lovely experience and I adored it. I loved the kneeling, it was a wonderful, uplifting feeling that I'd found the man in my life and we'd gone through all these games together and we deserved one another and that we were surrounded by people who envied this relationship, that was going to be a fruity, wonderful experience, with intelligence received on both sides, wit, every aspect of life would be celebrated equally between us. It was my favourite moment, Kate blossomed and her frustrations were thrown out of the window.'

Fiona Shaw, pursuing the more orthodox feminist line, was much taken aback by this and began weaving an argument about irony being implicit in the rhythm. Susan took off again:

'There's a certain amount of truth in woman's frailty. One feels bad when one is attempting to be something one isn't, and that it lacks grace and that it lacks the sort of relaxation in her whole temperament and person to allow herself to actually

---

[54] Eric Shorter, *Daily Telegraph*, 26.9.73

see someone clearly that maybe she can share her life with happily.'[55] Several reviewers had praised her delivery of this speech, one mentioning 'beautiful silky tones'.[56] She never took the chance to be simply and overtly aggressive when it was offered her in a role; when she had to, as with Regan, it depressed her thoroughly.

The part of Imogen makes other stringent demands. It was intensified by fiercely critical direction again, this time principally from Barry Kyle, with John Barton and Clifford Williams as associates. The text is far worse than *Pericles* in piling improbability upon improbability of plot. The language has frequent effects of bathos, with flat statements that militate against the romance. King Cymbeline, in particular, never knows what is going on. His exclamations, among many, can be played for laughs, and were, to great effect. Imogen, however, has to remain serious, to generate the radiance that alone can redeem the plot, and make her fidelity credible and moving. Susan did so, in a completely unqualified way.

'I remember her gentle hugging of herself with relief as Iachimo 'makes amends' by recanting his insinuations. This kind of inventive yet very natural touch characterised and enriched her whole performance ... Imogen's 'Why, I must die...' uttered neither in scorn nor in stoic acceptance but with the frank despair of one whose whole reason for living has been suddenly removed. Only such virtuosity can carry the actress through the appalling test of the awakening beside the headless body... Miss Fleetwood certainly succeeded in holding the theatre before the sense of the absurd could get out of hand.'[57]

She was helped by the silkily sinister tones of Ian Richardson, who as Iachimo set up the test on her chastity. He is half-way to Iago in credible evil potential. She is his counterweight. Doyne Byrd wrote:

> 'Her Imogen was very feminine, appealing but above all strong and that
> strength was, for me the hallmark of everything I saw her do. Backed, though,
> with an hysteria of matching strength. It made for a potent contradiction

---

[55] BBC Radio Three 15.10.94
[56] *Evening Standard*, 26.9.73
[57] Richard David, *Shakespeare in the Theatre*, CUP 1978, pp. 184-6

because the hysteria was never weak. Aware of her power I more than once heard her express her pride in being able to outvoice male actors and this was no delusion. Yet again in contrast to this forwardness she had a Diana Spencer-like retreating carriage of the head, with hunched shoulders, as if trying to reduce her imposing height ... her monologue over the dead Posthumous' had all the powerful mixture of strength and an affronted, almost girlish grief.' [58]

Irving Wardle thought her 'utterly consistent in the limpid openness of the role, and superbly in command of its broken, elegiac verse'.[59] John Barber said she was 'an ideal choice for Imogen. Her height and her bold incisive style ensure that the girl's innocence is not masculine. When slandered her candid and self-deprecating bewilderment is most distressing. Later with her hair cropped and disguised as a boy ... grumbling that a man's life is but tedious she is at once a creature lit from within by the lamp of her own integrity and, in her naivety, rather funny.'[60] Robert Cushman thought her 'fiery, witty and radiant'.[61] Benedict Nightingale wrote: 'Her Imogen is controlled and sentient, restrained and passionate. She makes us wait for her outbursts and, when they come, they hurt'.[62]

She won two particular admirers with her performance. One was Michael Billington, who wrote: 'Admittedly I have not always thought Susan Fleetwood had the weight for great Shakespearean heroines; but her Imogen moves from a graceful goodness to raw, naked grief with a power that shatters my opinion'.[63] The other was Duncan Heath, who had left the William Morris agency to carve his own career as an agent. He approached Susan directly at the stage door and asked if he could represent her henceforth. Moved by this troubadour-like stance, she agreed. It was a good choice, as she was eventually taken thereby under the wing of the top agency, International Creative Management. She was the first of a troupe of stars to come in under Duncan's battlements.

---

[58] Doyne Byrd, op. cit.
[59] Irving Wardle, *The Times* 5.6.74
[60] John Barber, *Daily Telegraph*, 5.6.74
[61] *Observer* 9.6.74
[62] *New Statesman* 14.6.74
[63] *Guardian* 5.6.74

The other plays that rounded off this stage of her career were Strindberg's *Comrades* and Gorky's *Summerfolk*. These are darker, even destructive roles, compared with the Shakespearean ones.

Comrades is, oddly, not translated as part of the collected works in English. Jeremy Brooks produced his own for this RSC production of 1974, directed by Barry Kyle. It deserves to stand alongside *The Father* as a discourse on marriage. The *Morning Star* said that Bertha (Susan) was the grown up daughter of Laura.[64] She is supposedly living as a comrade with her husband, Axel, 'bonily apprehensive and always looking one size too big for his clothes'.[65]

He gives her more than a fair chance to succeed in his line, as a painter. She argues that this is not enough, as, being a woman, she is already subject to many humiliations which he must share; this even extends to wearing a skirt. (David Thomas, in *Not Guilty* points out that whereas a woman can wear trousers and look perfectly feminine, the toughest sergeant-major would look but a fool in a skirt.) She is set to sabotage his career, and defrauds him on the housekeeping. She has an implacable will and no vestige of a conscience. Like her friend Abel, however, she is fascinated by the idea of a dominant male, who will be her equal in strength. When her husband briefly assumes this role, it produces immediate results:

> *Axel: What does 'love' mean to you? – isn't it just a cosy longing to be eating me alive again? Ha! Now you begin to love me! Why not before, when I was being good to you? Being gentle is being stupid so let's be rough with each other – is that what you're saying?*
>
> *Bertha: Well ... be a little rough, so as not to be weak. Oh, Axel, forgive me please! Don't give me up! Love me! Please love me!* [66]

This episode provoked different responses. One critic thought her 'too physically dominant'.[67] Another thought it 'a performance of bewitching subtlety (that) ...

---

[64] May Hill, *Morning Star*, 14. 10.74
[65] *Guardian*, 14.10.74
[66] *Comrades*, RSC Prompt copy, 3.8
[67] *What's On* 18.10.74

makes the monster female believable and even possibly more sympathetic than she should be'.[68]

Frank Marcus wrote that she 'never quite lost her brisk, no-nonsense Englishness, even when trying to entice her husband in ludicrous underwear'.[69] John Peter thought that Susan had chosen to play her basically as a person who did not know herself and where her energy came from; 'half mannish, half coltish, driven by nerves, half-understood ideas, and a powerful sexuality that doesn't quite understand itself until it is too late. One of the most rivetingly intelligent performances in London'.[70]

'I played an artist's model posing naked to Susan's amateur painter,' Doyne Byrd recalls. 'Little interaction was required of us in the short scene. She always demurely kept her gaze at my head level so I promised her sixpence if she 'looked' at the last performance. Her eyes dipped quickly down and straight back up again and I found sixpence at the King's Head bar.

During rehearsals for *Comrades* another quality was striking; her extraordinary naturalness. Her reading, discussing and acting were all of the same clarity and intensity and more than once she managed to confuse people as to which was which. *Comrades* also revealed to me the power of that hysteria when she chose to lie on the floor and rant about some unsatisfactory aspect of her relationship with the Peter Eyre character (Axel). She lay on her back with her knees up and apart in a wholly inappropriate black and red negligee which was painfully at odds with the hysterical energy coming out of her. For several of the company it was too much, but she stuck with it'.[71]

She herself said: 'I do have amazing energy, but it has been taxed over Strindberg's *Comrades* – it's so absolutely mad, the most *raw* emotions. I have found it the most naked-making form of acting, and it has been shattering to work on. I found myself having to think of how much one was having to disclose of

[68] John Barber, *Daily Telegraph*, 14.10.74
[69] *Sunday Telegraph*, 20.10.74
[70] John Peter, *Sunday Times*, 20.10.74
[71] Doyne Byrd, op. cit.

one's own identity, one's very personal thoughts. The nerve endings are exposed and quivering. I have even found it very difficult to learn the lines, which has never been a problem with me – difficult, I think, because of the content of the piece'.[72]

If work like this was hard and costly to her, however, that is not what the audience felt; they were witness to a creative triumph, in the portrayal of a struggling, incomplete soul. There was also a human reward to doing this play. She was to make a great friend in Peter Eyre and another in David Suchet, who played the writer, Willmer. This character briefly rebels against her authority, but it is only a spat. He comes back to beg forgiveness, and therefore won't even be a good partner for Abel. Her husband sticks out for another form of comradeship by the end, a kind of armed truce. He will pay the bills but see her only in cafes.

The lady in *Summerfolk* is less lethal, but more seriously unhappy. Martin Esslin pointed out that Susan 'discards the easy advantages of her youth and beauty, brilliantly characterising an ageing, hysterical old maid and blue-stocking: the over-intensity born of frustration with which she twists and turns, the false, self-deprecating modesty which is merely another aspect of her innate arrogance – these are not only observed with amazing clinical accuracy, they are also truly tragic'.[73]

Valeria is the literary lady in a house villa party, human territory made very familiar to us by Chekhov. Gorky, however, is closer in spirit to the revolution, although the play, of 1904, is only a few years beyond Chekhov. The characterisation of the bourgeoisie is harsher. The woodmen dismiss the summerfolk as being all alike, all shallow, transitory types, like bubbles. We see them as far more rude, scratchy, and given to venomous backbiting than Chekhov's people. Valeria cannot form even a temporary alliance with anybody. She has spent a lot of time on her own, thinking, and her ideas haven't been developed in discussion. She has a notion that ugliness is akin to something wrong in the soul. She doesn't anticipate the obvious comeback, that her physical

---

[72] 'Work as Therapy' op. cit.
[73] Martin Esslin, *Plays and Players*, Oct. 1974

imperfections can be seen in the same way. 'Redheads usually marry young' is thrown back at her, and she cannot manage badinage. She writes prose-poems, to be set to music. Her 'Edelweiss' recalls Trepliov's recitation about nature at the beginning of *The Seagull*. It is high-flown rhetoric, but with a core of emotion, in her obvious identification with 'the lonely little flower, the edelweiss'. Her voice grows desolate as she recites this closing line. The FT critic thought it 'the distillation of all that is gentle into verses of protective innocence. She reads them to a visiting author (Ian Richardson) who, in utter impotence of mind and spirit, sets the seal on this society'.[74]

The stage comments passed on it are vague but not unkind, and she flares up – 'Go away!' Later she advises Varvara to leave her 'vulgar' husband. 'You don't mind a bit of dirt. You get on with washerwomen. You could live anywhere'. It isn't meant to be hurtful, it could even be envy, but she can't reconstruct anybody else's life. Her observations aren't taken up by anybody. She admires the established writer, Shalimov, but they do not communicate. Ian Richardson recalls Valeria as 'perhaps the most wonderful of her characterisations'.

Their scene was 'full of very Russian inconsequentialities … a constant joy to play'.[75] 'When I go out of the house,' she says, 'I always take with me some sort of vague hope, and I always come back without it.' This got a deserved laugh from the audience, but it is true, and sad. At the very end, amidst general uproar and cursing, everyone having got too much on each other's nerves, she shrieks 'What about *me*?' It has the same effect as the maid saying 'Shall I serve supper now?' Nobody has any sympathy or insight to spare, although she won't be physically abandoned. It became a catchphrase humorously attached to Susan.

Susan was an excellent company member. According to such actors as Lila Kaye and Tim Piggott-Smith, it was easier to be so in those days, with more of a family feeling about the company than there is now, longer contracts and a more relaxed atmosphere. She enjoyed 'being part of a company where you work basically more for the whole than for the self'. Of the RSC she said: 'I'm sure I'm

[74] Anthony Curtis, *Financial Times*, 28.8.74
[75] Letter to author 21.5.99

more useful to them because I went away.[76] (of her Cambridge company excursion). 'I wouldn't like to work anywhere else at this time. I don't like the attitude, the people or the work that goes on outside – the idea of stars being gathered together for a single production. I like the people here, the community feeling. I'm not a person who plans things – I don't dream of playing any particular roles, and it rather suits me to be told what I'm going to do.'[77]

An interviewer asked her, in 1973, what her ambitions were:

'I do have a desire to work in film. But it would have to be something peculiar. I'm not a dolly bird. I don't fit any mould. I always sound older than I am. I'm in my mid twenties but I no longer say exactly, as agents and casting directors are so unimaginative when they see an age on paper. In a funny way I've always been middle-aged. I tell myself my real fulfilment will come when I'm slightly older. Perhaps in film.' [78]

Was she generally ambitious?

'Ambitious? Yes, I think I am. I'm not sure what the word means but I've come to the conclusion that being naturally retiring I must be ambitious to have remained so long in this profession. I have no special goal. No special parts I want to play. It's a day to day ambition of working well and doing a job as well as I can.' [79]

Ambition should be made of sterner stuff. Asked the same question in 1968 Helen Mirren said: 'I am massively ambitious. I have always carried around that view of myself as 'the star' in the Elizabeth Taylor, Sarah Bernhardt tradition. You know, standing in the middle of the stage in false eyelashes.' Mirren's wit does not detract from what she is saying. If she was Bernhardt, Susan was Duse. Of her own Cressida, Mirren said: 'I wasn't really sexy. I am fat, and I wore a low-cut

---

[76] Jane Evers, periodical undiscovered
[77] Frances Cox, *Plays and Players*, June 1968
[78] Jane Evers
[79] Jane Evers

dress.'[80] The *Sunday Times* critic mused that 'reputations have been made on less'.[81]

Susan was self-effacingly grateful for what she had. Acting, she said, 'is the thing which stops me going mad. I think the job is therapy for me. Without it I don't know what I would do – I think it would be something near madness. I am really very grateful for being employed. If I get time off, I really don't know what to do with it, and get the feeling that I'm never going to work again.' [82]

Susan referred several times to feeling as though she were always thirty. The actual year for this is 1974. One work of that year is interesting. It is a Granada TV play based on a story by Piers Paul Read, called *Childhood Friend*. Susan plays Janet Morton, a married lady, sociable and cheery to a theatrical degree, and engaged in the noble art of biography. She meets her childhood friend Alexander (Sasha) Tocharov, a successful English politician (played by Anthony Hopkins). They are drawn to revive the affair that barely got going when they were young. There is one affecting scene when they clutch hands over a table littered with books and papers, the tools of Janet's trade. She is in tears. Sasha has a very self-effacing wife, who turns out to be dying of cancer. She preferred not to let him know, as he cannot face up to very much reality. When she dies, Janet feels the full burden of guilt, and stops the affair. 'There's a life that's already been lived ... we're middle-aged. It's too late'.

To give those words authentically, Susan had to be another actress from the one who played Mary McDowell or Ophelia, although they were both only two years before. She looks quite different. The plump cheeks of youth and the sleepy expression in the eyes are gone, and Susan now has the look that she is to carry through life.

What had happened in between was her break-up with Terry, in 1972. Nobody I spoke to wanted to say very much about this.

---

[80] Trudy Procter's interview, *Daily Mail* August 9, 1968
[81] *Sunday Times* August 8, 1968
[82] 'Work as Therapy' op. cit.

'It was just too much,' one actress friend said. 'Six to dinner, iron my shirts and learn your lines for tomorrow.' It must have been her worst disappointment to date, however.

Her grief was undoubtedly genuine, but she had an odd way of coping with it. Doyne Byrd saw 'when she drifted among the company tearfully bewailing Terry Hands' leaving her to everybody and no one in particular. I was moved to make some comforting gesture. "Don't," I was warned. "She's always doing it. You'll only make trouble for yourself." It was hard to tell whether it was indeed an "act"'.[83]

She herself thought that she had 'a very deep craziness that is almost a madness. I'm far too emotional, far too subjective, and very often deeply depressed. I feel things with great intensity. When I'm feeling absolutely ghastly, I walk along the street and sing sometimes, and people say "You must be happy," and I say "You must be joking; I'm at my worst." When I'm feeling like this, and I hear and see people being happy, it makes me cry a lot, and I feel terribly in need of somebody to help me out of it'.[84]

Beauty in tears will always bring men running, but they aren't always wanted.

Looking back over her post-Everyman career to date, there is a somewhat pinched quality to it. The only full-blooded romantic Shakespearean role she had played with the RSC was Portia. There were victories with Marina and Imogen, but those ladies live in weird plays which will never be popular favourites. At the same age, Peggy Ashcroft had played a triumphant Portia and Imogen, and she had also been Perdita, Desdemona, and – several times – Juliet. Susan's romantic youthfulness had not been lived out on stage. Her remarks on Portia and Kate, however, show that on some level she carried the romantic ideal on intact. And she was ready for one of her new starts.

---

[83] Doyne Byrd, op. cit 30.1.98
[84] Ian Woodward 'Stars Ascending', 1973, periodical undiscovered

Part Three (1975-1986):

God's Little Golden Girl

V.   The National 1975-1979

IN HER INTERVIEW WITH PHILIPPA TOOMEY at the end of 1974, Susan said she could not see very far into the new year. An RSC tour was planned, to the USA, Australia and Japan, to end in May. 'After then is oblivion. I simply don't know whether the company will ask me to do something or not. I'd like to make a film, but that's pie in the sky ... ' [1] She duly went out to America, for the first time since 1964, with Ian Richardson, Mike Gwilym, Tony Church and Ray Wetherall to play scenes from *Summerfolk* and *Love's Labour's Lost*. The tour was abruptly curtailed when it turned out that neither Australia nor Japan would come up with the money the RSC was asking for. What were they to do?

Ian Richardson got talking to Professor Homer Swander, a teacher of English at Santa Barbera University, California, who had been bringing his students to England since 1967 to meet RSC actors. Estelle Kohler had dubbed him 'the grey-haired groupie' of the RSC. He didn't object to this, or to his other nickname, 'Murph'. He suggested that Ian Richardson, who had given seminars at Princeton, should come to California to talk to his students. 'How would you like five actors?' Ian replied. Homer was somewhat taken aback on the score of money, but not for long.

The Vice Chancellor of Santa Barbera was anxious to show that his university could host major events (a recent Beach Boys concert in the football stadium had incurred crowd trouble) and it was reckoned that the RSC contingent would not be so dangerously stimulating; 'Beach Boys Bring the Bard' ran the headline. They would do two weeks at Santa Barbera and one at Berkeley from the end of May, performing and running seminars.

From April to May Susan was performing *Love's Labour's Lost* back in England. The prospect of an American blend of showbiz and academia had her rattled.

---

[1] Philippa Toomey, 'Susan Fleetwood: Work as Therapy', *Times Saturday Review*, 21.12.74

Homer recalls her turning several shades of pale as it was put to her. Her patchy education came back to haunt her. She wouldn't do it, she said, unless Murph and Mike (Gwilym) came with her. They would. She was to field questions from a group of about a hundred women, of distinctly feminist hue. She threatened to go dressed as a bunny girl. She went, as herself, and was a resounding success; as were they all. Thus 'Acter' was born, an institution that still runs today, with a two-way visit every year. Susan came to call Homer's wife, Laura, her 'American mother', and became a great friend of his daughter, Beverley.[2]

It was a strenuous experience and Susan took a holiday in Hawaii with her brother Mick. Back in Los Angeles: 'For the first time in my life I felt I didn't want to work.' Peter Hall phoned her to invite her to come and work at the National Theatre. 'Oh God, another company job. The last thing I wanted was to tie myself down again.'[3] Perhaps her pleasure in being in at the beginning of things revived; or perhaps it was the absence of an alternative. At any rate, she went.

The National wasn't yet living in its South Bank home. With spiralling costs, endless labour disputes, and an appallingly hostile press, all recorded in nightmarish detail in Peter Hall's *Diaries*, the opening date had been put back from spring of 1975 to the spring of 1976. The company was still performing in its spiritual home, the Old Vic. Its history there had been celebrated on May 6th 1974 with *Tribute to the Lady*, a documentary by Val May for the Lilian Baylis Centenary, Peggy Ashcroft taking the part of Lilian. This was revived for the very last night of the company's tenure of the building – a 'cheerful, tearful end-of-term party' on February 28th 1976. Olivier, being ill, was only there in a recording of his Harfleur speech, but Richardson gave Enobarbus on Cleopatra's barge, and Gielgud delivered 'Oh, what a rogue and peasant slave am I', which he had first performed there in 1930. He was close to tears.

[2] Homer Swander interview 22.7.99
[3] Michael Owen, interview, *Evening Standard*, 1.3.76

'In the seat behind me,' wrote Felix Barker, 'Michael Redgrave – another great Hamlet, another Old Vic alumnus – was also close to tears. That was the sort of night it was, yet it never degenerated into sentimentality.' [4]

Peter Hall thought Peggy Ashcroft was 'like a reincarnation' of Lilian. She and Albert Finney as narrator went through all the familiar anecdotes to highlight Lilian's one-liners, ending with her addressing Denis Healey, then Chancellor, in the dress circle. 'What is going to happen to my theatre, the Old Vic? It is up to all you rich bounders to do something about it!'

Susan played her beloved Sybil Thorndike, who was present, aged 94, 'swathed in what appeared to be bales of muslin'. She 'turned round in her wheelchair, pushed flush against the stage, and cried out "Hello, everybody!" in a voice that shook the theatre to the very Gods.' [5] Felix Barker thought that Susan caught Sybil's 'emphatic spirituality'. The sound recording has her giving the lines with enormous relish:

An actress in the company said to me "We're always on hot bricks, aren't we? Lilian does keep us jumping." Her watch-word was that inspiring verse of the psalms – 'With the help of my God I shall leap over the wall.' Oh yes, she made us dance and jump and leap. [6]

Describing Lilian's funeral, Susan joyfully exclaims, 'There we left her – the fire, a symbol for her who was all fire and energy, the spirit, indestructible, living for ever.' [7] After this, Gielgud gave 'Fear no more the heat of the sun...' A spotlight picked out Susan embracing Sybil in her wheelchair. There was a real feeling of a torch being passed on from one generation to another.

Before that night, some National Theatre history had been written at the Old Vic. *Playboy of the Western World* opened there on October 29th 1975; *Hamlet* on December 10th and Osborne's *Watch It Come Down* on February 24th 1976,

---

[4] Felix Barker, *Evening News*, 1.3.76
[5] Simon Callow, *The National: The Theatre and its Works 1963-1987*, Nick Hearn Books 1997, p.44
[6] Val May, *Tribute to the Lady*, Typescript National Theatre Archive 1.19
[7] Val May, ibid. 2.13

before they all transferred to the Lyttleton. Bill Bryden, the young Scots director of *Playboy* promised Peter Hall a 'hard, precise, totally unsentimental'[8] version. He startled 'the Irish contingent' of actors who had come from the Abbey Theatre, P.G. Stephens, J.G. Devlin, Eddie Byrne – henceforth known as the 'Abbey Nationals' – by saying that he had never yet seen the play done properly. A recent Dublin production he thought had diminished the play by making it too folklorish. He wanted to make it a piece of truly European drama, going beyond what could happen in any closed community.

Some of the actors he had brought into the National, Mick McManus, Gawn Grainger, Derek Newark, Tony Haygarth, were called street actors, rugged and down-to-earth. (Peter Hall was to bring in Bob Hoskins.) The ethos was very male – beer and darts and football scores. Susan was the only woman in this set, and she was the only non-Irish member of the *Playboy* cast, although she had Irish blood on both sides of her family.

She was a great friend of Bill's; much enjoyed male attention; and spent five weeks in County Mayo to get the accent right. 'Poor, English Sue Fleetwood,' Peter Hall wrote, 'having to be a County Mayo girl in that company … But she read magnificently.'[9] The reviews confirmed that she got the accent. Peter Hall thought that in rehearsal it was turning out rather soft and sentimental. 'The stage is full of the Little People … as Irish as the Irish Tourist Board.'[10] He excepted Stephen Rea, Jim Norton and Susan.

Michael Billington thought that 'Susan Fleetwood's Pegeen has a delicacy and softness of skin that never suggests the rugged Irish coast, and although she is of good accent and discretion, the mournful, throbbing cadences of Synge's dialogue never seem a part of her personality.'[11] Several reviewers thought she made Pegeen too amiable. I saw this production and have no such memory. There is no escaping the ferocity of her preparing to burn Christy's leg to get him into the hands of the rural mob (who, if Brian Friel's *Faith Healer* is anything to

---

[8] Peter Hall, *Diaries*, ed. John Goodwin; Hamish Hamilton 1983, p.190
[9] Peter Hall, ibid. p.184
[10] Peter Hall, ibid. p.190
[11] Michael Billington, *Guardian*, 30.10.75

go by, haven't improved much since 1907). Her dialogue isn't mournful until the end; before that, it is rage or romance.

> *'Miss Fleetwood is a beautiful dreamer. Lying before the fire at curtain-rise she reels out an order for bridal clothes with the langorous longing of a self-appointed fairy princess; confronted a moment later by a prince who, in Mr. Norton's performance, bears definite traces of the frog, she unleashes her tongue to withering effect. She is a romantic scold – a combination that encompasses her changing moods throughout the play; when it ends as a burst of anger succeeded instantly by grief, it is seen to have described a neat and satisfying circle.'* [12]

B.A. Young, John Barber and Irving Wardle all liked it and Charles Lewsen was rapturous.

> *'There are nights when the stage breaks its bounds, unleashing a torrent of passion and joy. Such it was for me last night as Bill Bryden's production of Synge's intoxicating play now held us in rapt silence, and now caused us to laugh from our guts.'* [13]

Scheduled at first for 18 performances, it ran for 18 months, ending up in the Olivier. Susan was glad to have the specific approbation of Irene Worth, an actress she always deeply respected. After the first night, Maggie Whiting remembers 'meeting very proud parents … and being very much aware of the loving support there for her; her father, besotted with her. This warm and loving background gave us the actress we admired so much.' [14] Sue later swept into the first night of *Hamlet* on the arm of her adoring father.

This was a busy year for her. She moved into a flat in Greenwood Road, Hackney with Sebastian Graham-Jones, one of the National's directors. One of his little-used names is Peter and one of hers Maureen, so the new 'item' around was 'Pete and Mo' to those in-the-know. The flat was spacious – they called it 'Fleetwood

---

[12] R. Cushman, *Observer*, 2.11.75
[13] Charles Lewsen, *The Times*, 30.10.75
[14] Maggie Whiting, letter to author, 7.7.98

Towers' – but Sebastian's amiable spaniel would lie outside her door and sigh just often enough to disturb her fanatical concentration on her lines. In good weather she was out reading and sipping coffee on the balcony at 4 a.m.

They gave parties with music and wine. Susan was still eating and drinking heartily. 'She really is a golden girl,' her mother mused, looking on. 'Do not,' a close acquaintance was heard to say, 'let her catch you in the bath.' She evidently had all sorts of energy. 'I come tumbling into rehearsals awfully excited because I've got a new idea and just as I'm about to tell them I realise I'm in the wrong room telling the wrong people in the wrong play. It will only get worse.' [15]

Peter Hall had a wealth of talent to draw on for his *Hamlet*. Stephen Rea and J.G. Devlin as the two gravediggers 'virtually reprise their father-and-son act from *The Playboy of the Western World*.'[16] The brightest of his rough diamonds, Albert Finney, was to play Hamlet and Angela Lansbury was to take Gertrude; a singular choice, I suggested to one of the cast. 'Peter Hall's thoughts,' he replied icily, 'are his own'. Angela said of the production that it was 'extremely Anglo-Saxon. We were really rooted to the ground. It was very, very spare. At times, Albert resembled a kind of black-clad paratrooper and I felt like a rather rough-hewn chesspiece as the queen – chained to the ground.' [17]

I saw it, and agree with those who found Finney a glorious physical performer. There was little romance or poetry in the verse as he delivered it, but when he stood before the court after the murder of Polonius, firmly pinioned and about to be deported to England, he looked like a black cobra, vibrating with power, clearly perfectly capable, given time, of killing everyone on stage. Denis Quilley as Claudius had a honeyed voice that could have made you believe anything he told you and Susan was the most frightening Ophelia I have ever seen.

It was quite different from her performance of only three years previously and much more mature. She was a lady of the court to begin with, with a magnificent head of hair and a manner of brittle cheerfulness. This was discarded after

[15] Michael Owen, *News of the Arts*, October, 1975
[16] R. Cushman, *Observer*, 14.12.75
[17] Owen Falk, *Albert Finney*, Robson Books 1992, p.142

Ophelia goes mad; Susan then appeared in a white shift, her hair cropped brutally short. The effect was utterly shocking, as it always is when any woman is shorn. She pattered about in bare feet like a bird. The singing was cracked and distorted. She was hideously, convincingly mad. In rehearsal Peter Hall had noted, 'Sue Fleetwood in excellent state; instinctively she does wonderful things. She uses the circle of the stage as a garden from which she picks imaginary flowers to give to the characters she finds standing about her.'[18]

I remain astonished at the hostile critics of the production like Milton Shulman and Kenneth Huren, who were unconvinced. Others were moved: she was 'pathetically adrift in the early scenes and later … a harrowing image of a living girl who already has death in her face.' [19] 'There's a moment in which she gets down on the floor and sort of rubs her face into it. She turns into a kind of wild animal.'[20] Robert Cushman referred to Susan as someone 'for whose grace and power I am beginning to run out of superlatives.' [21] For the production as a whole, reviews were very mixed. Jack Tinker was scathing and Irving Wardle called it a 'ponderous cultural epic'.[22] But Michael Billington thought it 'sans question the best Hamlet since Redgrave's.' [23]

The last National play to come to light in the Old Vic was John Osborne's new play *Watch It Come Down*. Peter Hall and Bill Bryden believed in it strongly. Osborne was a star in his own right (Ken Tynan, at a gathering of National celebrities, said to him, 'come with us and make history!' – 'I've already made history,' was Osborne's reply.' [24])

> *'First reading of* Watch It Come Down *this morning; Osborne, looking curiously pink and strained, present. Bill Bryden made an incoherent speech, but it was engaging; his enthusiasm for the play bounded through like a great big puppy … it's a wonderful cast, and I think a powerful play. The first act*

---

[18] Peter Hall, op. cit. p.192
[19] John Barber, *Daily Telegraph*, 11.12.75
[20] Benedict Nightingale, 'Kaleidescope', BBC Radio 4, 11.12.75
[21] R. Cushman, *Observer*, 14.12 75
[22] Irving Wardle, *The Times*, 11.12. 75
[23] Michael Billington, *Guardian*, 11.12. 75
[24] Bill Bryden, interview 12.12.2000

has vigorous sardonic humour, and the second is one of the bleakest most terrifying I have heard outside Strindberg … Osborne has an amazing ability to draw into himself all the sicknesses of the moment…'[25]

The title was the advertising slogan of a demolition firm, applied now to the state of the nation. Some critics compared it to *Heartbreak House* and *Hay Fever*. A group of bizarre and highly-strung people, Ben Prosser (Frank Finlay) in films, Sally his wife (Jill Bennett), Shirley, a painter (Angela Galbraith), Glen, a writer (Michael Gough) and his gay friend Reynard (Michael Feast) and a girl called Jo (Susan) go to live on a disused railway station in the country, although the one thing they all agree on is that they loathe country folk, who kill their dog and end up blasting the station with shotguns.

Both the heterosexual and the homosexual couple are having very bad times. Jo is very fond of the aged Glen, and when he dies, she kills herself. Until then, she has tried to hold them all together with her unconditional affection. There is one moment of passionate embrace with Sally. When she goes, total destruction ensues. Osborne seems to suggest that when a cultural elite tears itself apart, the folksy, harmless English eccentricity that Jo represents won't be enough, and a lumpenproletariat will take over. From one angle, he is a nostalgic conservative.

The play certainly moved people. 'There was a bit of a riot,' Peter Hall wrote on February 20th, 'boos and cheers, and cries of rubbish and bravo. That's the stuff.'[26] Gillian Reynolds said that 'it was obvious from everybody's embarrassed shuffling throughout the audience that everybody was totally uneasy with the play.'[27] Both Peter Forster and all the cast, according to Michael Gough, felt that the audience hostility came from the same sort of people that Osborne portrays as the potential murderers at the end of his play. 'There were practically fistfights in the audience.'[28] Osborne hugely enjoyed the spectacle, and would bring in the hate mail to read to the cast, who developed an *esprit de corps* like troops in the firing

---

[25] Peter Hall, op. cit. p.206
[26] Peter Hall, op. cit. p.213
[27] 'Critics Forum', BBC Radio 3, 28.2.76
[28] Bill Bryden, op. cit.

line. At curtain call one night they burst out laughing at a lady in the front row who was chanting 'Money back, money back!'

Articulate opinion divided. It was dismissed as 'invective and gush';[29] 'full of acidity, dyspepsia and middle-aged yearnings';[30] and 'a wordy storm in a whisky tumbler'. One thought it a 'splendid finale' to the Old Vic[31] and Michael Billington found at least some of the writing 'a flaming emotional rhetoric that breaks through all one's English inhibitions about good taste'.[32]

All the reviewers, including the most unsympathetic, thought Susan the best thing in it:

> *'a special gold medal should be made for Susan Fleetwood's unflinching courage in the face of lines like, "He is breathing heavily in my heart".'* [33]

> *'If Jo is the heroine of the play, Susan Fleetwood is the heroine of the production: looking both subjugated and embattled, she attacks her mannered lines with flame-like sincerity that nearly burns her way through them...'* [34]

> *'Jo is played with quite outstanding warmth by Miss Fleetwood, and we feel that if the likes of her can only be permitted to live there is still hope for the world.'*[35]

Sue and Bill Bryden had figured out exactly the image that Jo was trying to live up to: 'Lend me that baggy cardigan,' she had said to her sister Sally, 'I have to play an earth-mother'. The figure of the hippy and beatnik hasn't changed very much over many a decade. Some reviewers thought that Jo was modelled upon Carrington, who could not endure the death of Lytton Strachey. If so, the part is idealised out of all recognition. Jo is not nearly so neurotic as Carrington, who

---

[29] Irving Wardle, *The Times*, 25.2.76
[30] Benedict Nightingale, *New Statesman*, 5.3.76
[31] R.B. Marriott, *The Stage*, 4.3.76
[32] Michael Billington, *Guardian*, 25.2.76
[33] Jack Tinker, *Daily Mail*, 25.2.76
[34] John Peter, *Times Educational Supplement*, 5.3.76
[35] Felix Barker, *Evening News*, 25.2.76

suffered constantly from bizarre nightmares, and whose suicide was fully expected. Bill Bryden rejects the idea. Jo is a version of the young Jill Bennett, who at eighteen had an affair with Godfrey Tearle, in his fifties. Glen is modelled partly on him and partly on George Devine. There was behind the scenes tension in that Osborne was breaking up with Jill, to take on Helen Dawson as his fourth wife. Rehearsals went well, however. Osborne worked tactfully with Bill and the actors. He was disappointed when the seventy per cent attendance was judged insufficient and the play closed. He never wrote for the National again.

Now at thirty-three, Susan was near the age she always described as her permanent state, spiritually, thirty or thereabouts. There was a certain serenity. She had of course entered the National as a leading lady, a status she had reached with the RSC. Not that she had any airs and graces; nobody did at the National at this period. She always enjoyed the ensemble spirit. 'So glad you're one of us now,' she said with great warmth to James Green, then a junior member. She met old buddies from the Everyman days: Kathy Alger, the wardrobe mistress, Michael Freeman, the director and Stuart Richman, the actor. Stuart remembers her looking steadily into his eyes and saying, 'Yes, you've grown more definite.' [36]

Michael Gough, 'Glen' in Osborne's play, was invited out to John Osborne's house at Edenbridge in Kent with Sue, where she heard Osborne say, characteristically, 'Think what you think – not what you ought to think.'

'But John,' she replied, 'think what you think, but don't always say it.'

Michael Gough became a highly valued friend from this period.

> *'When I first sighted Sue it was in the canteen at the Old Vic; she sailed in, tall and beautiful, wearing a vast white, woolly cardy. She moved as if she owned the place, without any conceit; it was just a fact that she owned the space she was in... In early rehearsals she was nervous, adrenalin bubbling. But once she had established a character and she knew who she was, she was fearless and bold.'*

---

[36] Stuart Richman, interview 23.3.99

Glen, the writer, is busy finishing his book for most of the first act, so Michael had to write something. At first he wrote out his lines, but Susan announced she was fed up reading them. 'So I wrote what I think is called a "stream of consciousness" – sort of freewheel thinking about the chaotic mess of my life which was going through a grim septic period. She never mentioned what I had written and so we never discussed what she had read. After one matinee, I heard her call to the prop man, "Where are yesterdays manuscripts?"

"You haven't kept all that filth?" I asked.

"Of course. I'm going to sell it to the News of the World."

"Don't you bloody dare!"

"As if I bloody would," she replied.

Of course I never for a moment dreamt that she might. We all of us would trust her with our lives... When we were in different plays at the National we used to send each other occasional notes. "Oh Susan Help! My nose is turning Blue." "Make up your face to match" she replied... Often she'd greet me with "Drop your shoulders and straighten your back. You don't have to be an old man all the time. Be proud." ... Memories of Sue come down in bits and pieces at all sorts of times of day and night and I am proud and blessed.' [37]

The character of Jo was drawn from these reserves of insight and compassion. The director Richard Digby-Day thinks that the suffering she had been through up to this period had drawn out her strength. Her emotional generosity was there on and off stage.

The other production of 1976, *Tamburlaine*, was chosen by Peter Hall partly to celebrate the origins of Elizabethan theatre, partly as another showcase for Albert Finney and partly (at a guess) in sheer defiance of the critics of the National's budget and the strikers who kept delaying openings. Five hours of non-stop triumphalism was what he needed. 'I sometimes wish that Peter Hall had chosen to baptise his new theatre with something less overwhelming than the Pacific

---

[37] Michael Gough, letter to author, 6.2.99

Ocean.'[38] The continual delays and the thought of the money they were losing brought him nearer to despair than had anything else. 'It's grave', he told the company, 'in fact it's absolutely bloody appalling.'[39]

On July 29th they all rushed out to perform in the open, where the technicians couldn't interfere, the first of several such occasions. Barbara Jefford recalls how difficult it was competing with traffic noise, including barges, and the odd drunk who of course felt like joining in. They had to pitch their voices very differently again, after the Olivier auditorium, which was already quite demanding enough.

In the play, Tamburlaine succumbs only to death. Albert succumbed to bronchitis, which stifles the voice and brings on general debilitation. He was pumped full of vitamins and hung upside down so that his chest could be tapped. When the play finally opened in the Olivier on October 4th, 'Finney not only survived the night, he flew'.[40] Reviews were very positive, although they all confessed that there was no avoiding the monotony of the piece. It is woven into the texture of the verse. Marlowe's reputation had been given a huge undeserved fillip by T.S. Eliot calling him 'prodigiously intelligent'; people assumed that a Harvard philosopher must know what that meant. John Gielgud was nearer the truth when he said, 'Do give my love to Albert. I think he's so terribly brave tackling that dreadful Marlowe, don't you?'[41]

Susan played Tamburlaine's queen, Zenocrate (four syllables, accent on the 'o' and the last 'e' – or she sounds like a three-syllable box). She is first his prisoner, and a concubine; as such she is as strident and boastful as he, but she becomes quieter, and falls in love with him, as he with her, quite obsessively. In rehearsals, she exclaimed 'Tamburlaine's a shepherd and I'm supposed to be a princess. How can I fall for him?' 'Ever heard of rough trade?' Finney replied.[42]

She said that she had known a relationship like this one, with the man treating the lady dreadfully, 'refusing to marry her until the very end when he feels he has

[38] Benedict Nightingale, *New Statesman*, 8.10.76
[39] Production notes, National Theatre Archive
[40] Production notes, ibid.
[41] John Heilpern, *Observer*, 19.12.76
[42] Production notes, op. cit.

done all he has had to do. Although she is hugely unhappy she still gets a big buzz from all Tamburlaine's power.' [43] Now, which of her directors, I wonder, most resembles a 14th-Century warlord? Her part is a bit like that of Jo, in Osborne's play, in creating a little oasis of calm amidst chaos, and pity against a welter of defiance and aggression, although of course she is compromised in that she benefits from Tamburlaine's conquests.

Reviewers thought that she transmitted that complexity. 'Susan Fleetwood achieved a look of wounded repose that is just right for a woman puzzled by her love for a bloodthirsty tyrant.' [44] 'Susan Fleetwood, a glass-eyed statue of disdain, speaking in horror of her lover's excesses.' [45] She aged impressively, from an empress to a little old woman, shrunk in death. The sound recording reveals her last speech to be noble and statuesque, without false pathos.

It was all somewhat stressful. Sue was meditating marriage and children, and looking forward to life after the National, 'to do film and some modern plays, something light – where all I have to cope with is a cigarette and one armchair on the set.' [46] She was not to get even near this until 1983 with a J.B. Priestley play, of which more anon. There was much *sturm und drang* to get through first. She felt the burden of being a company member, performing whatever came up. Her next modern piece, John Mackendrick's *Lavender Blue* (1977) took the role of the woman as victim to an extreme.

Mackendrick makes Osborne look like a model of restraint, and his plays islands of calm. A Yorkshireman and a public-school boy who had been a teacher, gravedigger, scrap-metal dealer, taxi-driver and family caseworker, he had written a thirty-minute monologue on nonentity called *No Hands*, which wasn't performed, and *Ludd*, a piece about the limits of love, in which a man mangles himself on a grenade; this was performed at the Ilkley Literary Festival in 1975. 'He distrusts the theatre and gets very irritated by actors,' noted the Yorkshire

---

[43] Vicky Maguire, *Daily Mail*, 4.10.76
[44] Milton Shulman, *Evening Standard*, 5.10.76
[45] John Barber, *Daily Telegraph*, 5.10.76
[46] Vicky Maguire, op. cit.

press.[47] This of course qualified him to be Resident Dramatist at the National. Susan's partner, Sebastian Graham-Jones was his director – and they did not get on. The play was not controversial in the sense that critics disagreed about it; they all felt a mixture of horror and contempt. Mackendrick blamed Sebastian's direction.

On January 17th 1977 Peter Hall noted:

> '*John Mackendrick, that mad, unhappy, talented writer whose play* Lavender Blue *we staged not long ago, committed suicide last night. I am appalled. Did its failure contribute to his unhappiness? I can never know, but I don't think so. He was hooked on unhappiness. I never heard him content about anything.*' [48]

In the play, Susan is Claire, a childcare officer with a caseload that includes Margaret, a mother of five, beaten up by her miner husband Jimmo, who urges her to get out and 'flog her hole' to get his beer money. Two children are at home, Arthur and Mary, who scream, sing and sexually molest each other. Another daughter, nine-year-old Kathy, we scarcely see, but she is understood to have met Peter, a deeply disturbed young man. They have sexual relations and he kills her for no particular reason. He then puts her dress on and walks the streets with her body. He is seen by Margaret; shrieks ensue; enter everyone.

Despite the contrivance, the essential facts are not incredible. I have heard social workers describe families getting up to things that could not be put on stage, even today. We never, however, get any insight into Peter's mind, or Kathy's, and our minds simply recoil in horror. The focus might be said to be on the social workers who are trying to cope.

As so often, Susan plays the longstop, the reliable pillar, the one who tries to keep everything going with her compassion. She rants against an uncaring society. Her dialogue with her clients consists of pure sympathy – 'whatever you want is all right with me, love' she says to Margaret, who wants a new home and money. She

---

[47] *Bradford Telegraph*, 4.11.77
[48] Peter Hall, op. cit. p.406

turns down her boss, Alan, as he is too bureaucratic and uncaring. She takes up with a younger, more cheerful man, Roy, a reporter, but after a vigorous fling, heralded by the notorious line 'lose me in the body-swamp again', she renounces him, too, to go back to Alan. She is thus always noble and self-effacing. She almost got away with it. 'Although she is lumbered with some of the worst lines in the play, she manages to suggest a woman of great compassion who is getting near breaking point herself.'[49] The *Times* reviewer couldn't go quite so far; 'however deep Susan Fleetwood is able to enrich Claire with an unscripted flirtatiousness, she cannot make the menopausal angel of the slums into a human being.'[50] One critic found her 'an irritating middle-class do-gooder. I did not believe in her at any time.'[51] Such a round condemnation is rare, and the fault lies in the writing.

In *Lavender Blue*, Susan plays a character who has to look on suffering she is helpless to avert. In Rachel Billington's TV play of 1979, *Don't be Silly*, she is at the centre of it. She plays Pamela Redman, a middle-class wife with two children and a husband, Michael, who has a good job, but fears losing it and drinks heavily. The story follows his steadily escalating level of violence towards her. He is a whining, nagging creature, constantly demanding sympathy. He smashes crockery she is carrying after an argument that has blown up out of nothing. They go to Brighton for a weekend, but their lovemaking is interrupted by Pam thinking that someone is listening through the thin hotel walls. He is furious, and gives her two black eyes, claiming that he thought she was about to attack him.

It almost becomes a joke when he orders a raw steak for breakfast, to put on her eyes. Her friend Ellie calmly takes it as a joke, too. 'I never knew Michael had such zing in him.' The play portrays female insensitivity, as well as male. Her mother insists that she is exaggerating. Professionals, the children's headmistress and the family doctor (Stephanie Cole) sense that something is wrong; the headmistress says that the children act as though they come from a deprived home, alternately clinging and aggressive. They don't have time to avert the

---

[49] Charles Sener, *Surrey Daily Advertiser*, 11.11.77
[50] Ned Chaillet, *Times*, 11.11.77
[51] A. Seymour, *Yorkshire Post*, 11.11.77

outcome. As Pamela is cooking frozen peas, Michael condemns them as 'frozen muck' and pulls her arm so that she scalds herself. She has the chance to throw the rest of the water over him, and we wish she would. Although tall, he is of slight build, and makes one feel that if Susan were to exert her strength, she could knock the skinny little bastard into the middle of next week. His hold on her is psychological. The actor, Charles Godwin, has a hideous gleam in his eye, the kind of effect that Bruce Dern does very well, suggesting manic willpower divorced entirely from self-knowledge. His last attack on her is without any pretext at all. He begins to hurt her in bed and when she complains, says 'Your body is more important than my mind, is it?' As she gets up to see to the children, who are crying, he chases her into the bathroom and beats her savagely. Her screams are bone-chilling.

The last scene of the play is also the first, a hospital interior seen from the viewpoint of a patient on a trolley. Her last line is amazing: 'It's my fault. I just couldn't help annoying him. It's my fault.' Earlier she had said 'He wouldn't be bothered to hit me if he didn't love me … he's my whole life'. Clearly her mindset has something to do with her inability to avert his attacks. Her infinite passivity is what enrages him.

After it was shown (BBC 2, July 24th 1979) there was a panel discussion, which turned on the feasibility of this happening in a middle-class home; it was a radical suggestion then. The detail of the argument over the frozen peas is revealing. The husband is like a successful middle-class male who pretends he is living in a George Eliot village, with Mrs Poyser in the kitchen. He wants every modern convenience, but the woman must work as she did back in those days. Fay Weldon portrays this type well. Pamela has no ideology to support her, feminism not being such a force in the land in 1979.

It is interesting that the female television reviewers of the day brought out Pamela's weaknesses. 'She was one of those gently complacent women who boast about their non-violence, and defend their whims with soft implacability… forever souring the enjoyment of her husband and making it plain that the children's interest always comes before his.' [52] Philip Parker said that she was always 'puncturing the romantic moment, remembering to do the right thing at the wrong time, taking the blame as the easier way out.' [53] So convincing was Susan's portrayal of the battered wife that she was asked several times to address groups on the issue. She had to explain that she was 'only' an actress.

The assertive side of her nature came out when she was Hilda, in a three-part TV version of L.P. Hartley's *Eustace and Hilda*. She is an independent woman of the world in the twenties, an administrator and very bossy to brother Eustace. Her emotional life remains suppressed. One moment from it is beautifully caught from the book, when she runs along throwing confetti at the wedding of sister Barbara. The laughter and tears together distort her face movingly. Desmond Davis, the director, wanted to catch the poetic qualities of the book, the fateful events, visionary insights, the power of memory. Hilda is actually resistant to this. She denies having had an idyllic childhood, she is brisk and businesslike, and she is not at all drawn to the high life, as is Eustace. Getting the better of her in discussion, for once, Eustace gets her to the English country house, Anchorstone, where she meets Dick Staveley, played by Tim Piggott-Smith. The wild side of her character emerges as she plays a rough version of billiards with the young set, yelling, her hair a-tumble, whacking the ball with her hands, which get scarred. Later she goes flying with Dick in his biplane, and after the very late landing which has got everyone worried, she makes an imposing picture coming through the dusk in her flying jacket, hair just released from her helmet, glowing with the sense of adventure. At night Eustace dreams of going to see Hilda in her room. Dick is there.

There is a long shot of Hilda in the nude on the bed, rather hazy, in keeping with its being a dream. Susan prepared for it thoroughly, as ever, using an ice cube to get her nipples up. Her expression is striking, very straight and serious, not at all coy. Tim Piggott-Smith made his nightgown look like a Roman toga as he haughtily dismisses Eustace. What exactly ensued in the affair between Dick and Hilda isn't clear in the book. Her will is described as stronger than his, but she

---

[52] Sylvia Chaplin, *Daily Telegraph* 25.7. 79
[53] Philip Parker, *Sunday Telegraph* 29. 7.79

wanted to depend upon him in a way he couldn't meet. It is odd that this should result in bodily paralysis. What is clear is that when Eustace gets her out of this, her deepest emotional life is concerned with him. Both of them have let reasonable prospective partners go. They end with a kiss that she deliberately makes very sexual. She is back to her bossy self, ordering him about, but what she will do in the future for a man remains a mystery.

Plays of an earlier period gave her other chances to spread her wings. She was on Radio 3 on December 20th 1979 with Ian McKellan as Torvald and Michael Gough as Dr. Ranke, in Ibsen's *A Doll's House*. The chemistry between them all is excellent. As Nora, she enjoys the jokes she shares with them both in the early part of the play. She growls with pleasure about her forbidden macaroons, and giggles at the idea of shocking Torvald by saying 'bloody hell' to him. Her theatricality is calculated. She is manipulating both men. McKellan plays Torvald not just as a stuffed shirt, but as a highly irascible, volatile man, with no emotional centre. Her mind works fast and well on the facts of their situation, as they unfold. At the end she confronts him, stage by stage, with her dawning realisation of their predicament, and his authority collapses. Susan eliminates all the melodramatic suddenness of this with the surprise she registers at her own emotion.

She was another Nora in 1977, in O'Casey's *The Plough and the Stars*, directed by Bill Bryden. Often Nora is played as a little waif, but there is already one such in the play, Mollser, played well by Nora Connelly. Bryan Murray (the young Covey) said that Susan played her Nora like a lioness. The text certainly allows for that. When she denounces her husband as a coward for going back to the barricades, fearing his mates' contempt, she is speaking straight from O'Casey's heart. (The Captain Brennan who taunts Jack is actually pretty good at looking after number one, as Bessie notices). Nora is capable of terrible rage:

> *One blasted hussy at a barricade told me to go home an' not be thryin' to*
> *dishearten th'men … That I wasn't worthy to bear a son to a man that was*
> *out fightin' for freedom … I clawed at her, an' smashed her in th'face till we*
> *were separated …*

In terms of acting, Fluther and Bessie are the hero and heroine of the play, off the barricades, but Nora is at its heart. She is pure tragedy, whereas comedy prevails elsewhere in the play, even at the end, with the banter between Fluther and the cockney soldiers. There is a grim, stoic quality behind the flowery language. These are the urban counterparts to Synge's peasants, with their 'queer joys'. They will always be arguing, speechifying and shedding blood. Someone said that the Irish may be great talkers, but nobody ever listens.

The reviews were pretty censorious: about the production drowning in the wide spaces of the Olivier (which the actors from the Old Vic did find a big challenge); about the accents and even about Susan as 'a second-rate Ophelia' in a part that 'scarcely allows the actress a way in' – 'embarrassing' – 'she was bad, really' – 'totally incomprehensible.' [54] As regards accent, J.G. Devlin (Peter) said, 'You have to water down a Dublin slum accent or half the world wouldn't understand a word you said.' [55]

The actors, Tony Doyle (Jack) and Carmel McSharry (Mrs. Gogan) found Nora very moving. According to Sinead Cusack, Cyril Cusack (Fluther) was a terrible perfectionist and he was well satisfied with Susan. Bill Bryden heard him say to Sue and Tony ('the children', as he called them), that, having seen the play and performed in it all over the world, their version of the love scene was the finest he had ever seen. Coming from a grandee of Irish acting, that meant a lot to them both.

I have only heard a sound recording of the production, but that had the power to move me to tears. I have never heard such pain in a human voice. The hostile critics sound like blind and deaf ghosts. Bernard Levin referred to:

> 'an amazingly foolish woman on the radio [Maeve Binchy] who declared
> that, "O'Casey was cynical about war and cynical about love" – she no doubt
> believes that Mozart was tone-deaf and Renoir colour-blind... The two who
> fight their way into the truth are Susan Fleetwood as Nora and Cyril Cusack
> as Fluther. Nora is an almost impossible part, with a mad scene more

[54] Maeve Binchy, 'Kaleidoscope', BBC Radio 4, 21.9.77
[55] J.G. Devlin, interviewed by Raymond Gardner, *Guardian* 20.9.77

difficult than Lucia di Lammermoor's, and there is only one way for an actress to bring it off: to close her eyes and run along the tightrope. This Miss Fleetwood does; she pours love as a severed artery gushes blood, and never stops for a breath of self-consciousness. The consequence is a performance of rare quality that tears at the heart and burns in the mind.' [56]

Yes! And thank God for one reviewer with some fire in his belly and words to his pen. There was praise also from Michael Billington and Benedict Nightingale, who said that Susan transformed the play 'into what it finally is, a tragedy, one of the barest fistful of 20th Century plays to merit the name.' [57] It makes one realise how difficult it is to write about such a personal and fleeting an art as acting and how uncertain that profession is when marvellous performances can be so disregarded. (It took Bernard Levin's pen, again, to make people realise how good the RSC's *Nickleby* was, when it should have been obvious to everyone.)

Peter Hall decided to direct *The Cherry Orchard* in June 1977. His confidence was shaken by the news that Peter Gill would be putting his version on at the Riverside, Hammersmith in February 1978, just before the National production. When he saw it, his admiration was qualified, 'Chekhov the way the English like it, not particularly funny and not very passionate.' [58] He would try for both of those qualities.

'Rehearsed 'The Cherry Orchard' Act I all day. Sue Fleetwood is actually making Varya funny. It's clearly what Chekhov wanted. The characters are all funny. They are totally egocentric, living their own fantasies. They avoid emotion by changing the subject. They hear what others' problems are, but don't listen; that would be dangerous. They therefore emerge as quite ruthless with each other. It is very Russian, unsentimental and un-English.' [59]

---

[56] Bernard Levin, *Sunday Times* 25.9.77
[57] Benedict Nightingale, *New Statesman* 30.9.77
[58] Peter Hall, op. cit. p.331
[59] Peter Hall, op. cit. p.327

He would have a star-studded cast: Dorothy Tutin as Ranevskaya, Albert Finney as Lopakhin and Ralph Richardson as Firs. Nevertheless, when Bernard Levin gave the Riverside version a rave review, he was alarmed.

> 'First night of The Cherry Orchard. The cast seemed in high spirits but very nervous. I tried to say something of what their support had meant to me, and nearly, I regret to say, burst into tears... The atmosphere in the auditorium was as cold as could be. In the air was not – How is this Cherry Orchard? It was – Here is the latest disaster from the National Theatre because they can't possibly live up to the Riverside production. I am not dreaming this; it is not my paranoia; I have never known a more hostile house. It says much for the cast that by the second act they had gripped the audience and by the end had scored a bit of a triumph. My gratitude and admiration for them is boundless.' [60]

On the Sunday he notes 'ghastly reviews from Levin and Cushman'.[61] Levin in fact greatly admired Albert Finney and thought Susan's Varya 'a complex and fully human study'.[62] He thought that the characters' isolation from each other was an accidental lapse, rather than an interpretation. In general, it was thought at least the equal of the Gill production. Billington thought that Varya was like Sonya in Uncle Vanya. (She is also like the Sonya in War and Peace, the adopted girl, very much a fifth wheel.)

> 'Hall has one lovely directorial touch when, during Charlotta's conjuring tricks, everyone applauds wildly as Anya is revealed behind a rug but shows absolutely no interest when Varya is similarly discovered: that says it all. And Fleetwood and Finney play perfectly the scene where they are thrown together for the expected proposal; her face at first is all bright-eyed expectation which, as he gazes steadfastly out of the window, crumbles into disbelief. Fleetwood, forever jangling keys with the irritation of the totally reliable, has done nothing better.' [63]

---

[60] Peter Hall, op. cit. p.336
[61] Peter Hall, op. cit. p. 337
[62] Bernard Levin, *Sunday Times*, 19.2.78
[63] Michael Billington, *Guardian* 15.2.78

Chekhov described her as 'weepy and rather stupid' and Susan would play her that way, avoiding the temptation of exploiting her pathos. 'I wore a terrible wig that looked like a Brillo Pad and I had a kind of Vaseline effect around my nose, as if I had a permanent cold. Poor Varya, she's such a victim.' [64]

Several reviewers thought Susan the heart of the play. Jeremy Treglowan, for instance, praised the:

'...unselfish warmth of Susan Fleetwood, whose Varya goes a long way towards anchoring this otherwise drifting production. It's hard to imagine a less ostentatiously tragic performance than hers, or one which manages to stay so sympathetic while giving Varya her full share of bossiness and nerves. Many of Fleetwood's best moments are taken off the other actors – her embarrassment at Lopakhin's boyish enthusiasm for his plans to turn the orchard into a holiday resort, her struggle to control her sympathetic tears when Trofimov's arrival overwhelms Ranevskaya with the news of his pupil, her dead son.

At the party, Fleetwood plays Varya's emotional states with marvellous assurance – shrieking excitedly in the dances, irritated with everyone in between times because she is worried about the expense of it all, painfully humiliated by the general lack of interest when Charlotta produces her from nowhere as the second human rabbit in her conjuring trick. The list could go on, but it would have to end with the non-proposal scene, in which Varya's unglamorous niceness and Lopakhin's deeply-concealed lack of self-confidence rush round together like a soup that won't thicken. In a touching, extremely funny moment, Albert Finney, a trapped frog staring around mindlessly, blowing out his cheeks and bolting at the first opportunity, to leave Varya helpless in tears on the pile of family luggage, one more unneeded bag on the heap.' [65]

Robert Cushman thought her the best Varya he had ever seen. 'It's a beautiful study of frustration and frustration at being frustrated, and of self-induced

---

[64] Interview with Vera Lustig, *Plays and Players*, Feb. 1991
[65] *Plays and Players*, April 1978

anger.' [66] Nobody compared her to Valeria, in *Summerfolk*. On paper, they are very close. There is repetition in the stock of characters in Russian plays and novels. It is hard to tell just how much of an advance in acting Varya was for Susan. Bearing in mind her words about her happiest times being with Chekhov, one's guess is that hitting Varya with such accuracy must have given her much pleasure.

Back in 1976 a dream had been spun of a general Don Giovanni season at the National, including Moliere and Shaw. By 1978, all that remained of this was von Horvath, an Austro-Hungarian playwright who produced his *Don Juan Comes Back From The War* in 1936. It is an ensemble work, with thirty-five women oscillating about the Don, who is looking for his first love, whom he admits to having abused. His old spell still seems to work effortlessly; he charms lesbians, older women, and young girls, although they all tend to turn on him in rage after a while. The grim postwar times are making them hard. He floats about society with plenty of money. One girl gives him a job as an art dealer, then he becomes a speculator. At the end, he finds that his beloved died in 1916. He seems quite ready to expire on her tombstone.

It is a wispy play, as though the author had begun to sketch in a statement about the changes brought about by the First War, and then decided to leave it as that, an impressionistic sketch. Twelve actresses took all the parts in Stewart Trotter's production. Susan played a café lesbian, a communist party member and a dentist. All end up furious with the Don, and in her first persona she made her scene 'the most arresting of the evening' by stabbing his photograph. Time and again critics say that Susan was the best thing in a production, whether a good or a bad one. Reviewers were generally kind to this one, but it sounds like a museum piece. 'Just what is this play about?' Susan asked the director; she never thought she got an answer.

In August of 1978, Edward Bond was given the Olivier on which to stage his epic piece *The Woman*, in two parts, lasting three and a half hours, with a cast of 43. It was his own version of the legend of Troy, to comment directly on our own world,

---

[66] Robert Cushman, 'Critics' Forum', BBC Radio 3, 18.2.78

its politics and warmongering. Bond approached the National with suspicion, thinking it part of 'the Establishment' in another guise, with limited tolerance of dissent. 'I am a member of the working class. When I go into, let us say the National Theatre to work, it is as an inmate going into an institution. I have absolutely no doubt about that ... We need to use the National Theatre facilities and machinery for our purposes – not anyone else's. We must not come as captives in a Black Maria. We must come to the National Theatre with the same artistic and political imperatives we carry elsewhere – and come prepared to fight for them in the National Theatre as anywhere'.[67]

He began by interrogating the actors on their politics. 'Derek Thompson said he was to the right of Ghengis Khan. Bond sniffily pointed out that this was not original.'[68] 'He was out to rattle everyone's cage', Sebastian observed.[69] One might have thought that after witnessing the trouble John Arden and his wife had brought to the RSC, and Mackendrick to the National, and with a context of bloody-minded industrial action, the patience of 'the Establishment', i.e. the subsidised theatre, had been stretched to bursting point. Those were the days when members of the Socialist Workers' Party strode into actors' dressing rooms, demanding to know what they would do when the revolution came. Hanif Kureishi made a satiric portrait of this kind of actor with Terry in *The Buddha of Suburbia*.

Bond's piece was much more coherent than *Island of the Mighty*, but it was demanding. He wanted 'a new sort of acting'. It had to follow the writing in being clear, moving from one image to another, clarifying issues. As a true Marxist and in theatrical terms a Brechtian, he distrusted emotion. People were to be judged not by their feelings or emotions but by their ideas. Anything else was dangerous. This has consequences for acting. He found the company 'still belonging to the nineteenth century. The company were acting emotion, having feelings in themselves, gazing on themselves, speaking to themselves even when they shouted. They were private performers on a public stage, still part of the

[67] Malcolm Hardy, 'Edward Bond: England's Secret Playwright', *Plays and Players*, June 1985
[68] Peter Hall, op. cit. p.342
[69] Sebastian Graham-Jones, interview 7.11.2000

bourgeois theatre.'[70] Peter Hall had a row with him on May 3rd, accusing him of seeking confrontation and not taking any time to motivate people into playing small parts. By August they were seeing more eye to eye. Bond's final verdict, however, was that he'd have preferred to do the play with an amateur company who would have followed 'the political bias of the plot. And there was no way I could get that understood at the National.'[71] Susan wasn't alone in thinking that he just didn't understand actors.

The Woman is Hecuba, played by Yvonne Bryceland, whom Bond called 'the greatest living actress'.[72] She strikes up a relationship with Ismene (Susan) when she comes to Troy on an embassy. It occurs to Ismene to offer herself as a hostage to ensure the peaceful departure of the Greeks, after they have got what they came for, a statue of a goddess. She throws herself into a pacifist role and proclaims this loudly to the Greeks from the wall. She joins with Hecuba in calling for Astyanax, Hecuba's son, to be brought up as a Greek, but no, he must die, and Troy must be destroyed to satisfy the Greek rank and file. Ismene's husband, Heros, disowns her, and hopes that once she is bricked up inside the wall – the punishment for treason – she will eat poisoned food and die quickly.

In part two, she has been released and is living with Hecuba on an island. Hecuba has torn out one eye, in protest against the murder of her son. Ismene has lost her mind, but is very quiet about it. A delegation comes from Athens, looking for the statue still; allegedly it has been lost just off the island. A lame refugee from the Athenian mines shows up, to fall in love with Ismene. This brings the women to deal with life again, and there is a tender scene in which Ismene unveils Hecuba's good eye, only to find that she is totally blind.

They now feel like mother and daughter, however. Ismene says to the man, 'Since you've loved me my mind's begun to clear'. Hecuba persuades Nestor, the head of the delegation, that Heros, the real nuisance obsessed with the statue, has lost the goddess's favour, and deserves death for losing a race with the miner, who duly despatches him. Hecuba dies in a storm. Ismene can be left with her new

---

[70] *Plays and Players*, October 1978
[71] Malcolm Hardy, op. cit.
[72] Malcolm Hardy, op. cit.

husband in a rural idyll. According to Bond, Hecuba shows 'the need to use violence to create socialism out of capitalism ... I have represented history as a woman with a sword under her skirt.' [73]

As with Brecht, the humanity we see on the stage does not fit the cloudy allegory the playwright likes to contemplate. No reviewer understood what the whole purpose was, but there was much praise for individual performances, such as the petulant Heros (Nick Henson) and the grisly Nestor (Andrew Cruickshank). It is moving to contemplate the desperate shifts the women are driven to, in the name of sanity, in part one. Hecuba was judged 'a shrewd and witty woman driven to specific desperation'.[74] Ismene had 'the right urgent sanity'; she was generous and 'emotionally unguarded'.[75] Her 'tormented idealism... has a beauty that transcends the material in which she works... her Greek princess into peasant girl is another triumph for a progressively fine actress'.[76]

Roger Gartland recalls rehearsing with Susan; 'the crippled man has to grab her at one point. I hesitated. Sue immediately grabbed my arms and put them round her saying most vigorously "Oh come on!" To get to the point of the work was for her everything.'[77]

Susan and Yvonne Bryceland were great friends. Both could bear the full weight of great classical roles. Bond's play is fine enough to be called half-way to this. (His *Lear* got much further in building a bridge between ancient and modern literature, in a very rare achievement). The dialogue makes no concession to charm or local colour. Billington called it 'pugnaciously aphoristic',[78] with quirky, usually grim comedy, and flashes of real insight. It has the same quality as Bond's essays, however, of arising from a mysterious depth of solitude, and rarely connecting with the people and situation actually to hand. The characters become emblematic and, as Robert Cushman put it, 'oddly weightless'.[79] Susan

---

[73] *Socialist Challenge* 28.9.78
[74] Michael Billington, *Guardian* 11.8.78
[75] Michael Billington, op. cit, and Irving Wardle, *The Times* 11.8.78
[76] J.C. Trewin, *Illustrated London News* 29.9.78
[77] Roger Gartland, letter to author 7.6.98
[78] Michael Billington, *Guardian* 11.8.78
[79] Robert Cushman, *Observer* 13.8.78

felt that it was a powerful vehicle, although she had no idea what it all amounted to. 'I've always been selective over the parts I play', she said in 1980. 'I have an instinct that tells me what to do and what not to do. Whenever I've gone against that instinct I've regretted it. A play hasn't been right or I didn't get on with the director. I've learned to obey that instinct.'[80] One imagines that having happened once or twice at the National, although the cracks were papered over.

[80] Peter Mc Gary, 'On Stage', *Coventry Evening Telegraph* 11.4.80

VI.   Theatre, Film & Television 1980-1986

IN 1980 SUSAN RETURNED TO THE RSC to play one of the roles she was born for, Rosalind in *As You Like It.* The whole production was conceived by Terry Hands on the basis that she was available; he celebrated her 'enormous vocal range, technical range, unequalled in England at the moment. I can't think of anyone abroad, either.'[1]

With sets by Farrah, Sinead Cusack as Celia, Joe Melia as Touchstone and John Bowe as Orlando, it was a resounding success. Sally Aire declared:

> 'I have never seen him direct with so much generosity and warmth. Farrah's
> design, too, has an uncharacteristic ebullience ... Susan Fleetwood's
> Rosalind is the pivot, and this must surely be the definitive Rosalind for this
> generation of actresses. I have not seen Rosalind better played; I don't expect
> to see her better played for a very long time, if ever ... There is bubbling
> humour and that human warmth which has always been Susan Fleetwood's
> greatest natural quality as an actress'.[2]

The play was taken pretty fast and furious, not at all as a slow pastoral idyll. Orlando was highly excitable throughout. The sensuality was very strong. 'Susan Fleetwood's Rosalind can scarcely keep her hands off John Bowe's Orlando and Celia is man-hungry, quite capable of picking up Orlando should Rosalind ever consider dropping him'.[3] Rosalind is highly strung, her emotions coming thick and fast. Often she feels not in control of herself, an effect achieved, of course, with a great deal of work. She absorbed Terry's numerous suggestions. Her listing of the attributes of Time, or of a lover, are delivered at breakneck speed, and the line 'One inch more is a South Sea of discovery' has 'inch' as a yell, and a laugh fluttering in 'South Sea'. When she denounces Phoebe she is vehement, tremulous in referring to a good man's love, and arch in calling her an article 'not

---

[1] R. Miles, 'Theatre Call', BBC Radio 4, 9.4.80
[2] Sally Aire, *Plays and Players*, May 1980
[3] Sally Aire, op. cit.

for all markets'. Irving Wardle noted her 'tremendous emotional range and speed of transition ... achieving her next change before you can anticipate it'.[4] One reviewer noted her 'constant switching from the ludicrous butch tones of her disguise to the trembling vulnerability of a woman lost for the first time in the wonder of love'.[5] The butch tones are used after the news of Orlando's encounter with the lion.

Terry Hands thinks Rosalind the female equivalent of Hamlet. If so, this must extend to his melancholy. In this vein, Jacques carries the seriousness of the first part of the play into the forest. He is given a lot of scope. Michael Coveney said that Rosalind was 'strangely drawn to Jacques'.[6] He embraces her and gives her a red rose. In the dialogue about travel, she is infected with his melancholy, sympathetic at the notion that experience could 'make me sad, and to travel for it, too!' The marvellous speech, 'No, faith, die by attorney ... ' was very quiet and serious. The laughter at the 'foolish chroniclers' was sad, and the line 'these are all lies' was almost tearful, as though she momentarily disbelieves in love. I don't know why she should be so angst-ridden. Jacques is sentimental-melancholy, and she packs him off in Act Four scene one, to get on with Orlando. She can be played a touch more like a Restoration heroine, suave, relaxed and amused in the badinage with Orlando. Terry Hands would not have it so.

Allan Hendrick writes that 'her portrayal of Rosalind was full of love and joy that seemed to me to be utterly true and unaffected. She gave every one in *As You Like It* a first night present of a heart, made from corn husks and tied with a green ribbon. Mine is hanging still on my kitchen wall'.[7] One of her admiring spectators was Roger Michel, then working in the bar of the 'Dirty Duck', Stratford, but destined to be Susan's director years later, in *The Buddha of Suburbia*.

It is interesting that John Barber, who described Sue as a 'chestnut-hair beauty bounding with health' also said that 'this actress seems formed by nature for tragic

[4] Irving Wardle, *Times*, July 24, 1980
[5] Charles Spence, *New Statesman* July 23, 1980
[6] Michael Coveney, *Financial Times* July 23, 1980
[7] Allan Hendrick, letter to author 5.5.98

parts … One watches her heart in mouth'.[8] This year was in fact more tranquil for her than the storm-tossed seventies. (One recalls a background of the three-day week, the miner's strike, a cod war, and disaster movies.)

'Sometimes I wish I had allowed myself more time for other things in life. I'm not married and I don't have any romantic involvements. I suppose I've just not found the time … My career has been and is everything to me. I've come close to having a relationship occasionally, but I suppose I've always stopped myself before it came to anything.' [9]

She was directed by Terry Hands again in 1981, in *Pleasures and Repentances*, an ensemble piece on romantic love, inspired by *The Hollow Crown*. It was first conceived in 1967 and in its lifespan toured the world. Susan appeared as Jane Austen, Queen Victoria, Fanney Burney and Anne Boleyn, rounding off the evening with a deadpan recitation of the Rolling Stones number, 'I Can't Get No Satisfaction'.

In the romantic vein, Susan portrayed another woman surprised by love in a radio version of *Eugene Onegin* in 1980. The story follows the skittish, wandering nature of Onegin. It is strongly coloured by Prokofiev's music, a world premier for a score thought lost, but rediscovered and orchestrated by Edward Downs. It is autumnal music, broody, slowly revolving, with just one or two bursts of happy lyricism. Susan's voice runs parallel, conversing with her nurse and trying to get the impossible Onegin into serious discussion, and then rising once or twice to an ecstatic level. As Tatyana, she is said to be not so pretty as the conventional young heroine Olga, beloved of Lensky, the poet; but she has all the best lines.

In 1982 she was Titania in *A Midsummer Night's Dream* directed by Bill Bryden, 'a very distinctive director', as she said, ' a tremendous inspirer of people. He uses an awful lot of energy himself. You have to watch him just as much as you have to listen to him'.[10] For his part, Bill wanted a star for Titania, which was Susan, and he got another in Paul Scofield, who wanted to be Oberon. 'Sometimes,' says

[8] John Barber, *Daily Telegraph* July 23, 1980
[9] Peter McGarry 'On Stage', *Coventry Evening Telegraph* April 11, 1980
[10] *Bath Evening Chronicle* November 30, 1982

Bill, 'one and one make three'. At first things didn't go well. Everyone's style was different from everyone else's. Sue had reverted to an official RSC style, not at all sexy or sassy and the mechanicals weren't funny. Scofield said it was the worst read-through he could ever remember.

Bill knew what he wanted, however. He was trying for an English sort of charm, with the fairies as ghosts from an Elizabethan house, to make the production wholly unlike Peter Brooks' famous version, which had been more like a Chinese circus. There were platforms and ropes in this one, with fairies abseiling down to the stage, but the effect was different. It opened in the small Cottesloe, some people paying £1.50 extra for a cushion to sit on the stage. Some were firmly displaced by Theseus, when he and Hippolyta needed their thrones to be center stage. Musicians on stage played Victorian music hall ditties as an introduction.

When it was to transfer to the Lyttleton, Susan said 'I think it's a wonderful celebration. We're going to try and keep all that enchantment'.[11] John Barber, Michael Billington, Francis King, Robert Cushman, Irving Wardle and James Fenton were impressed; Michael Coveney, Milton Shulman and Jack Tinker were not. Billington's point was crucial; 'it brings the world of the mortals and fairies into ever closer and more harmonious contact'.[12] Titania, Susan thought, was 'very sensual', although she baulked at the word 'earthy'.[13] Irving Wardle described her as an 'ageless Persephone figure, even when winding her legs round those of the sleeping Bottom'.[14]

What I remember of this production is the spectacle of her amazing legs, emerging from something like a grass skirt. It speaks volumes for her delivery of the verse that I felt drawn to that, too. It was ecstatic at times, to such an extent that it ran the risk of sounding absurd, had the strength of her conviction not defied this. John Barber said of Paul Scofield's Oberon and Sue's Titania that 'they make every speech poetic and every word treasurable'.[15] 'Even in the first

---

[11] Brian Matthew, 'Round Midnight', BBC Radio 2, 5.4.83
[12] Michael Billington, *Guardian*, November 26, 1982
[13] Brian Matthew, op. cit.
[14] Irving Wardle, *Times*, November 26, 1982
[15] John Barber, *Daily Telegraph*, November 26, 1982

confrontation with Oberon there is a very sexual feeling, because they accuse each other of flirting with mortals'.[16] 'Susan Fleetwood's Titania shamefully confesses to responsibility for natural disorder'.[17] The element of sensual wickedness was a new quality to her acting. Francis King thought she had 'much of the langorous glamour of a vamp of the silent screen'.[18] In her scenes with Bottom, she is always very much the queen. 'Tie up my love's tongue; bring him silently' was firm as well as rapturous, and the line 'Out of this wood do not desire to go' was a command, not a plea, delivered with a narrow, intense concentration. He is a prisoner of demon-fairies, as she thinks, forever. Scofield was the very senior Oberon to deliver her from this illusion, 'The contrast between a half-disembodied Mr. Scofield and an extremely earthy Miss Fleetwood is one of the strongest elements in the production.'[19] Scofield thought that Sue's Titania was 'a thing of beauty, marvellously spoken, and of infinite grace, a grace that was her gift and characteristic'.[20]

This year she again emphasised her single-mindedness:

> *'I'm always amazed and faintly envious when actors manage to get married and have children and think about schools and houses and weekends...*
> *Because I lead a rather solitary life I'm good on energy; when Terry Hands and I broke up it was still possible for us to go on working together in the theatre, I suppose because that was what had brought us together in the first place. You can do so much with directors you know and love, but in the end all that matters is the acting.'* [21]

As regards the acting, it had occurred to her that Shakespearian heroines, however triumphant, wouldn't make her famous.

> *'I suppose it's just that I've always lived the company life, never wanted to go out into the marketplace and test my luck. I know that as a result I'm really*

---

[16] *Bath Evening Chronicle*, November 30, 1982
[17] Michael Billington, op. cit.
[18] Francis King, *Sunday Telegraph*, November 28, 1982
[19] James Fenton, *Sunday Times*, December 12, 1982
[20] Paul Scofield, letter to author November 5, 1999
[21] Sheridan Morley, *Times*, Jan 9, 1982

too little known for the work I do and I know that I might be more useful to the RSC if my name could actually tempt people into the Theatre the way that, say, Helen Mirren's does. But I'm just not very famous and there's not a lot you can do about that until the right television comes along.' [22]

When she got to it, her television work in this period wasn't very distinguished, apart from *The Good Soldier*. There was some excellent stage work to do, anyway.

In 1983 she was to work with Bill Bryden again in a simple piece of charm, *Cinderella*, the National's first attempt at a panto. She was very excited by it, according to Alfred Lynch. It was conceived, again, in a Victorian and Edwardian tradition, with cockney songs like 'boiled beef and carrots'. It was extensively reviewed. William Dudley's sets were universally praised, as were the real ponies drawing Cinderella's electrically-lit coach, and, of course, Susan's legs. (Any panto whose Principal Boy's legs are inferior may be written off.)

Her singing was less awesome. Billington praised her 'secure bottom' – 'if you'll pardon the phrase' – but said she had a 'shaky top'. [23] John Barber was enthusiastic. 'London has not seen a lovelier panto in years. Susan Fleetwood, wearing white satin tights and a smile to dazzle the gods, gives Principal Boy a Byronic dash slightly salted with humour.' There was also a very tight corset that was a considerable endurance test, so the dazzling smile was bought at a cost. Barber also wrote, however, 'I wish I had not found the atmosphere so confoundedly chilly'. [24] Other reviewers echoed a sense of estrangement. James Fenton thought it 'has all the beauty of a Victorian toy. May we play with it, the audience asks, or may we only admire it from a distance?' [25]

The rapport with the audience was insecure. There was an oft-repeated story of one child who caustically remarked that Cinderella's gown (a tablecloth) needed a belt, and of another, who when Button asked winsomely if he should read Cinders a poem he had written, robustly replied 'no'. The production was praised

---

[22] Sheridan Morley, op, cit.
[23] Michael Billington, *Guardian*, December 17, 1983
[24] John Barber, *Daily Telegraph*, December 17, 1983
[25] James Fenton, *Sunday Times*, December 18, 1983

for avoiding adult-joke vulgarity, but it was said to lack the right kind of earthiness that does attract kids.

If charm was subtly blended with danger in *Midsummer Night's Dream*, it was surrendered for overt danger in *La Ronde*, of 1982. This came out of copyright at the end of 1981, sixty years after its first Vienna performance. A rash of productions broke out, at the Royal Court, The Brighton Rep, the Manchester Royal Exchange and the Aldwych, where John Barton directed Susan's RSC company, with a translation provided by Sue Davies. He regards the play as a modern masterpiece, not a boulevard comedy, although Michael Coveney thought that he hadn't, in fact, made it any more than that. It is modern in its preoccupation with language, as in a Pinter play like *Betrayal*, where language as the characters use it is never to be seen as even capable of expounding truth.

La Ronde was done as a period piece, Vienna of the twenties, with dancing waiters. It was rehearsed at great length, in separate scenes, the actors not generally mingling. Susan played Emma, the young wife. She is deceiving herself with a very conventional seducer, the young gentleman, who has just enjoyed the parlourmaid. Constantly demanding reassurance and threatening to go away, never to see him again, she in facts stays and makes love for hours. With her husband, she is very calm. He insists that women must be pure, and that all affairs can be conducted as fantasy, inside the bonds of marriage. Impure women all die young. His wife indulges his ramblings and transparent cover-story; in the next scene he is busy seducing the 'sweet girl'. She knows the falsity of both men, but never challenges. Irving Wardle wrote that 'Incredulous, abrasive and mocking lines are always breaking in, threatening to explode in the face of her smug menfolk'.[26]

Sara Mason, who played the parlourmaid, recalls:

'La Ronde is a very sexual piece and many of the actors had great difficulty in making the sex act seem real. Not Susan. In the bedroom scene, her eyes would close, her head move backward on the pillow, and then her face and

---

[26] Irving Wardle, *Times*, December 1, 1982

body would shudder. You could absolutely see the moment of penetration (her face would shudder), followed by the exact moment of orgasm. She had no inhibitions, either, she just performed her part naturally, realistically, without shame or comment. Her performance was fluid and very physical ... She had less rehearsal hours spent on her scenes than any of the other actors, perhaps the director thought she didn't need the rehearsal time ... We spent far longer working with the choreographer on her bits than with the director ... She moved like a dancer. I got the feeling she thought through her feet. Although the way she used her voice was also unique. She would almost sing her lines, to a kind of tune in her head, accompanied by movements that were carefully worked out and performed like a dance in time to the rhythm of the music in her head. The result was captivating to watch ... Like a ballet or modern dance.[27]

Susan was no less robust in speech than in performance. When asked by Trevor Hyatt on Thames TV what she thought the play was about, she replied 'the social and sexual games before and after fucking'. There were 150 protest calls. She refused to back down. 'There really should not be all this fuss. I was describing sexual intercourse without love, so you cannot call it lovemaking. What do you call it? I make no apologies to anyone.'[28]

She played a different kind of sexual creature in Ayckbourn's *Way Upstream*, which opened at the National in August 1982. There had been a year's delay. The play called for a 24-foot cabin cruiser to float and move in a 6,000-gallon tank of water on stage. 'I hate to say there's a jinx on this play, but certainly we have had a lot of bad luck with it,' said the stage manager.[29] When a similar project had been tried once in Texas, the stage manager had had a nervous breakdown. A Fred Karno production of 1910, with a boat on stage, had flooded out the audience when the tank broke. Ayckbourn's plot is basically a sitcom on the theme of the disastrous holiday. Most reviewers thought that an allegory had been superimposed on this. Keith, the ineffectual businessman and group leader,

---

[27] Sara Mason, letter to author September 8, 1997
[28] *Sunday Telegraph*, January 15, 1982
[29] *Evening Standard*, December 13, 1982

abdicates to the stranger Vince (Tony Haygarth), a capable boatsman, but the incarnation of evil. As an old-fashioned spiv with a wide streak of violence, it is hard to see what his allegorical significance might be. He takes over the boat, and a decent young couple, Alistair and Emma, are driven to violence to get in back. Ayckbourn was brooding on the desperation some people felt about living in the eighties. One review said that it was 'as if *Three Men in a Boat* were taken over half way through by the Marquis de Sade.' [30] Susan, as always, took it all very seriously.

> '*What he writes is so much a document of our times, the way people speak and the way they behave. He speaks about us. It's also like being with a computer ... The play is like an intricate piece of machinery in its precision. The temptation is to think that because it's modern it isn't all that precise. Then someone changes some tiny word and you realise that it just isn't as good, and you very quickly go back to the word he wrote. He's terribly aware of the sound and rhythm of words. Working with him in rehearsals is intimidating, but when I'm just going around being myself I feel that his powers of observation are like laser beams, and that he's watching me and classifying me.*'

She thought him a 'living legend' [31] and for his part, Ayckbourn was well pleased with her.

> '*I tend to avoid actors who claim to have a gift for comedy. The best comic actors are generally the best actors full stop. They play the truth and let the comedy take care of itself. Well, almost. Although* Way Upstream *has its comic moments, it certainly isn't without its dark side. I needed someone playing June who would take us way beyond the world of light comedy. Hers is a very dark journey. Susan had the power I was looking for and wasn't afraid to play the shadows ... She was a hard worker, I remember that. Always anxious to get on and try it again and again. I liked that. Rehearsals were just fine. We all got on and, though it was a varied group – Tony*

---

[30] *Event*, October 14-20, 1982
[31] Ray Connolly, *Standard*, August 6, 1982

Haygarth couldn't have been more different in his working methods than Sue for instance – in a day or so people seemed to be working well as a team. By the end of the four week period we had a very strong show.' [32]

Brassy vulgarity doesn't spring to mind as Susan's forte, but she managed it splendidly for this occasion. She plays June Taylor, Keith's wife, a 'one-amp brain' as her creator put it,[33] a 'slovenly sexpot', 'delightfully raucous' with a red hennaed wig; a 'sex-starved suburban housewife'.[34] Several writers compared her to the infamous Beverley of *Abigail's Party*. She has a showbiz background with a singing group called the Ginger Nuts. Flattered by Vince's attention, she sings for him, shrill and horrible. Susan had her own theatrical streak, which she put on for fun, in company. She drew on it for June, for a later series of glossy media ladies with bored, drawling voices, and finally for the supreme prima donna, Anna Arkadina. June was also drawn from a mother Sue once saw on a holiday ferry who said sepulchrally to her child, 'You're going to do an infinite amount of damage with that ice cream!'[35]

June is quite ready for a bit of 'naval discipline'. There is some suggestion of play with ropes when she and Vince go below deck. She goes along with all his escalating violence, and in her final appearance, on Armageddon Bridge, she is nothing less than an evil harpy. Most of the time she spends in a bikini which made her freezing cold night after night, however:

'This is by far the most technically ambitious play I've ever been in. The wretched boat bobs about on water on the stage for the whole play, and when it rains it really rains for fifteen minutes every performance.' [36]

Changing costume was done inside the boat, and she was a bit frightened of all the tumbling about inside and out of it. She was alternating June's part with that of Titania, and the gold make-up she wore for that, interacting with the cold and

[32] Alan Ayckbourn, fax to author May 4, 1999
[33] Ray Connolly quoting Ayckbourn, op. cit.
[34] Benedict Nightingale, *New Statesman*, October 8, 1982; Ronald Hayman *Times Literary Supplement*, October 22, 1982
[35] Interview with Sally Fleetwood, March 19, 1999
[36] Ray Connolly, op. cit.

the wet here, gave her an infection. Being a vamp can be tough. She delighted, however, in showing off her amazing figure in her bikini, to the raucous joy of the stagehands; male approbation, alas, is not a subtle thing. She was almost universally praised, artistically, as the best and funniest thing in a doubtful show. Phrases like being 'in deep water' and 'up the creek' abounded. After finishing with this and the 'Dream' she left the National, declaring: 'I'm up for sale. It's a big adventure!' [37]

Her television appearances in this period were not her biggest adventure. She played a series of wives. There is Lady Caroline, a society hostess in the 1983 series *Strangers and Brothers*, married to Roger Quaife (Anthony Hopkins) and doing her best to further his career despite his adultery with Ellen Smith (Anna Calder-Marshall). She upbraids him and refuses at first to divorce him because she loves him. The dialogue is very stilted and C.P. Snow's men are all appalling stuffed shirts.

In J.B. Priestley's *Dangerous Corner*, a play of 1932 adapted for television in 1983, she played Frieda, adulterous wife to Anthony, who ends up killing himself after losing all his illusions about family and friends. Sara Badel (who played Olwen) says that Sue put her usual great intensity into the role, so much so that a blood vessel burst in her eye.[38] This and problems with the set brought filming to a halt just where Olwen makes her great revelation, that she shot the man who had been obsessing everyone. Nobody could spot the break from the finished product. Susan wears a long, silvery period dress, with bare arms, shoulders and back, which makes her look enormously powerful. She handles a cigarette holder very elegantly. These things stay in the mind long after her dialogue, although laden with revelations like everyone else's, has faded.

She is an embittered wife, Charlotte, in *The Blue Dress*, a play in 1983 from a story by William Trevor. She rejects her husband Terence (Denholm Elliot) as impossible to live with. She had just one scene in which she is making up, looking very modern and smart in trousers and sweater, to go to a party with

---

[37] Brian Matthew, 'Round Midnight', BBC Radio 2, 5.4.83
[38] Sara Badel, phone interview October 21, 1999

another man. Terence's main fault is to dwell on unpleasant truths, which destroys his relation with the gloriously youthful and pretty Dorothea (Felicity Dean), who seems like a gift from the gods until the murderous secret of her childhood is revealed.

In the Granada series *Travelling Man*, directed by Sebastian Graham-Jones, (1985) Sue plays Carol Sheridan, wife to an honest farmer (Julian Glover) who is suffering from rustlers. She appears behind a stranger, the hero Lomax (Leigh Lawson) with a shotgun, which she very quickly lowers and breaks open, confessing that she's never fired it. Lomax wins her trust very quickly. She seems to meditate having an affair with him, confessing that her life is dull, but after rounding up the rustlers he goes on his way, like Shane, seeking for he who hath wronged him. Peter James made a neat, and violent thriller out of the television scripts by Roger Marshall. Susan looked good in country garb, tall boots and thick jackets, baling hay and driving a tractor.

In *Murder of a Moderate Man* (t.v. version of 1985), a spy thriller with a very complex plot, she plays Annie, a sympathetic lady who wants to help the innocent refugee escape from an ubiquitous Arab killer. He catches up with them, and the refugee is killed sitting on the back seat of a car beside her. She is spattered with his blood.

Her films of this period are much more interesting. There is one fine piece of hokum in 1985, *Young Sherlock Holmes*, directed by Steven Spielberg. This deals with the schooldays of the young detective. He correctly deduces murder as the cause of death of a number of amiable gentlemen. A dart from a blowpipe causes them to have illusions that drive them to suicide. Special effects of course come in with the illusions. Young Watson is hit, and believes he is attacked by a whole shop-window full of cakes, but Holmes saves him. The assassin is none other than Susan, cunningly covering for herself with her day-job as Dribb, the school matron. She is a priestess in an Egyptian death-cult, which has a huge wooden underground temple. Holmes discovers them about to mummify a maiden. Scores of handsome, robed, bald-headed young men stand about chanting something that sounds like 'it's ninety-nine, it's ninety-nine hobbit'. These are inhabitants of Wapping, Michael Hordern's voice-over tells us, driven mad by social deprivation; well, with just Millwall as their football team... Susan is bald and be-robed, too. She has a dart blown back at her from her own pipe, and as if that weren't enough, staggers away in flames, as the wooden temple burns.

The part of the reliable longstop had come her way before, with *Clash of the Titans* (1981, director Desmond Davis). In the collection of goddesses, she plays Athene, goddess of wisdom. Ursula Andress was on hand to be Aphrodite; enough said. Susan hardly moves at all. She stands, looking statuesque, holding Bubo, her owl, symbol of her wisdom. Her face lights up with a sly smile as she announces her idea for keeping him out of the dangerous venture proposed by Zeus (Laurence Olivier). He is replaced by a mechanical owl, a jolly little fellow who tumbles about most amusingly, and was a big improvement on the real Bubo, who during the shooting dug his claws into her shoulder, nibbled her ear, demanded mice continually, and crapped on her dress. She wasn't bothered by this, and proposed to carry on shooting – 'It's out of camera, isn't it?' – but Thetis (Maggie Smith) objected. 'But it's there!' she proclaimed, disgustedly.

Susan unfortunately didn't get further than Shepperton studios; she was not needed for the Mediterranean sequences. The film was a lot of fun to make, Olivier regaling them all with his bawdy stories. It was harshly reviewed. The models, the last ones to be articulated by hand, before computerised and digital images came along, are impressive, and the film was at least as entertaining as *Jason and the Argonauts*.

In 1981 Susan played a leading role in a television film of the Ford Madox Ford novel *The Good Soldier*. This is a study of the lives of the international super-rich in the years leading up to the First World War. Imaginatively, we have been accustomed to see this period through a golden haze of nostalgia. The lush costumes and venues were admirably filmed by Tony Pierce-Roberts, in Nauheim, Holker Hall, Croxteth Hall, Stanway House and Chetham's Library. The people live in the utmost luxury, but unhappily.

> '*No, by God, it is false! It wasn't a minuet that we stepped; it was a prison – a prison full of screaming hysterics ...*'

The stresses and strains of the period are in fact apparent in many of its works. As a great admirer of Henry James, Ford probably drew some inspiration from *The Golden Bowl* (1904), to which his unexpected description of the characters as hysterics would also apply. (James Ivory has by now filmed this, too). Of the hero, Nancy Banks-Smith astutely observed, 'The sad thing, in retrospect, is realising how enormously Ashburnham, who died in effect from boredom, would have enjoyed the war.' [39] This is one theme of many a novel of the war, including Ford's own *Parades End* sequence and Richard Aldington's *Death of a Hero*; that men go to war to escape from their wives.

The wife here, Leonora, is played by Susan as a formidable creature. 'She defined the word presence,' Robin Ellis says of Susan. He sensed a coiled quality within her, of possibly volcanic emotion. [40] In the role, her imposing stature is fully felt. One review described her as 'an ocean liner of a lady, but with the hidden stabilisers shorn away'. [41] Her relaxation and charm as a hostess give way to a terrible anger when she is upbraiding her husband, played superbly by Jeremy Brett as an upright, inarticulate figure, who cannot explain his perpetual womanising even to himself. Passing one of his mistresses in the corridor, Maisie Maidan, she gives her a hell of a clout on the head, pretending to be adjusting a clasp for her. Her rage at the last beloved, Nancy (who never becomes a mistress), is compounded by real jealousy.

It is Nancy's purity that keeps her husband fixated, and Leonora wants to keep her in the house to torment him with somebody unattainable. Both women are committed Catholics, but whereas Nancy is orthodox, Leonora keeps offering bargains to people or to God. (The element of casuistry in the book was part of its appeal for Graham Greene, whose own *The End of the Affair* would have been a wonderful vehicle for Susan.) Ideals must never be admitted to have failed, they must be constantly re-applied. 'Am I never to have a chance?' is her best line, delivered before a burst of grief. After Edward's suicide, she marries the only

---

[39] Nancy Banks-Smith, *Sunday Telegraph* , April 16, 1981
[40] Robin Ellis, phone interview November 29, 1999
[41] Russell Davies, *Sunday Times*, April 19, 1981

other presentable man she ever met, determined to enjoy love and a normal life, a choice which, in this context, still looks forlorn.

Leonora brought Susan two other parts from two famous directors, James Ivory and Tarkovsky. Ivory admired 'the complex woman of the Ford novel... the intelligent and attractive wife, in her smart black evening dress'.[42] In the Merchant Ivory 1982 production of Ruth Prawer Jhabvala's novel *Heat and Dust* she was to play 'an official British matron, close-minded and closed off to the Indians she had to deal with in her official duties ... She gave Mrs Crawford a sort of jittery, nervous laugh and fixed smile – fixed against all the horrors of Indian life she encountered. She was not an attractive figure and the Indian Nawab, played by Shashi Kapoor, made fun of her and compared her to a hijara – the dancing eunuchs. But Susan was game and carried the part off – rather like Mrs Crawford herself had carried off all the things she came up against [although] ... unlike Mrs Crawford she loved being in India and enjoyed making the film.'[43]

Susan was Beth Crawford, the Burra Memsahib, wife to the Collector (Julian Glover). She has five scenes. In three of them she is trying to correct social gaffes made by Olivia (Greta Scacchi), the young heroine who ends up by creating a serious scandal. She slips her a handkerchief for her to spit out a stone from her dessert at a ceremony. She spreads twittering dialogue over Olivia praising the Begum's son too fulsomely when they are being received by the Begum and her ladies, and she amusedly advises her not to go to hear the music after a feast, that being usually just for the men. Olivia takes in none of this. She is much better friends with Harry (Nickolas Grace), the Nawab's favourite, but then so is Beth. She comes in upon Olivia and Harry singing 'I Pagliacci' and joins in, horribly, collapsing into giggles after a line or two (it was a shared joke between Nickolas Grace and Sue that neither of them could sing a note). She has come to give practical advice on travel. She refers in passing to Mr Ghandi's lot 'stirring things up again – they never miss a chance!' Her knowing little school-prefect laugh is a

---

[42] Letter to the author from James Ivory, December 16, 2001
[43] op. cit.

well-observed piece of Englishness, inviting the others into a complicity of disapproval.

At the end, after Olivia has run off to the Nawab, she turns this sort of laughter against Olivia, to the extent of saying she was probably quite a good sort, but her 'embroidery and piano would hardly do for Satipur'; adultery naturally followed. Beth keeps up a fixed, determined glare even while drinking tea. Although she speaks the language, Beth is never seen interacting with Indians. James Ivory never attempts to portray India from the unknowable Indian point of view. He shows Europeans interacting in that background, and making sense of it as best they can. Some retire defeated, like Chid and Harry. Beth Crawford is quite secure inside her limitations.

Susan might have made a good Memsahib. She learnt some Urdu before going and questioned her teacher closely on the status of Indian actresses and the state of the film industry out there. Along with Nickolas Grace and others, she got amoebic dysentery as soon as she got out there and they all had to stay in reach of a lavatory during the shooting. Some of the makeup girls went home immediately. Susan and Nickolas were shocked by the poverty they saw on the way in from Bombay airport, but thought better of Hyderabad, when they saw it later. Susan discovered the joys of cheap fabrics, crimson silk for about twenty pence a yard, and the virtues of lassee as a safe drink. She was profoundly affected by the country, as anyone must be. Old Rajahs' palaces were opened up just for the film and the company went to see the Taj Mahal by moonlight, a spectacle which moved her to tears. When filming was over she was joined by Sebastian and they travelled together. Later she would travel there alone, quite an endurance test for a lone woman.

James Ivory said of their films, 'I feel that *The Europeans* is Ruth's, *Quartet* is mine and *Heat and Dust* is Ismael's.' [44] One wonders in what sense. The glossy appearance of the film and its leisurely pace belie what went on behind the scenes. Pay was precarious. 'When the electricians' money ran short, Ismael offered them daal and rice. "We don't want your fucking daal," they said, "we

---

[44] John Pym, *The Wandering Company*, BFI Publications 1993, p.64

want our fucking money, and if we don't get it, you don't get no fucking picture'. They took to wearing T-shirts saying *We work for curry*. Ismael professed outrage. "This is a reputable company!" Actors went to bed not knowing whether they would be shooting on the morrow. Notes would come under the door to say yes they were. Cheques had cleared.' [45]

Susan's perennial problem had not gone away. At first James Ivory 'sprang all sort of surprises on her' with new or changed lines. 'Later, somebody advised me to be more careful … she was dislexic and had trouble reading … I didn't know this at first'. [46] It was surmounted.

In Leonora, Susan had played a passionately, tragically serious lady. It was this quality that made the famous Russian director Andrei Tarkovsky choose her to play the hero's wife in his last film *The Sacrifice*. The scene in *The Good Soldier* in which she enters the dining hall, sweeping along in a low-cut black dress, was enough to hook him, although he interviewed many actresses from all over Europe.

At 53 (in 1985) Tarkovsky had achieved a European reputation for his five films, beginning with the Golden Lion award at Venice in 1962 for *Ivan's Childhood*. This enabled him to work outside Russia, where he had grown increasingly exasperated at the incomprehension and disapproval of his work from the authorities. He was no sort of explicit dissident, in those days predating glasnost, but the poetic and introspective qualities of his films did not fit the criteria of soviet realism. Popular response was mixed; some were bewildered by his art, but some said it spoke to them intimately. He always said that his work was simple enough for children to understand, but he has become a somewhat esoteric cult figure since his death, in both East and West.

By 1984 he was a confirmed exile, suffering from separation from his son, whom the authorities would not allow abroad. It was perhaps some compensation for him that there was almost a family atmosphere about the group of people he had carefully picked for *The Sacrifice*, including Erland Josephson for the hero

---

[45] Nickolas Grace, interview August 24, 1999
[46] Letter from James Ivory, December 2001

Alexander, and Bergman's photographer, Sven Nykvist. Not that all went smoothly – as it rarely does in families. His methods and Nykvist's were much at variance at the beginning, but after 'sniffing one another out in an animal way' as Susan put it,[47] they got on fine.

She said of Tarkovsky that the whole cast 'adored him in a way which knows he is a bloody nuisance most of the time, but that he is still wonderful.' Layla Garrett recalled Susan on the set as 'totally professional: she was always on time, she never complained, never whinged at the weather or Tarkovsky's time-wasting, such as when he was experimenting with a pool of water, completely forgetting his actors. Her reaction would be "So what? We're not filming a soap opera. We're working with a difficult director who happens to be a genius."'[48]

Susan herself said:

'I was never in the least worried or intimidated working for him. Some of the cast were, I know. But for me it was simply a privilege. He was so exciting to be with. I felt he was giving me enormous scope to express emotion, to do what I wanted with the part. It is an extraordinary thing, but I felt totally in tune with him. It was like ESP. Often I found that just a few seconds before he asked something of me, I knew what it was and reacted. But there was one minor crisis which helped to establish our relationship. It was when, during a scene, he came over and moved me a bit harshly and impatiently ... I got annoyed and I caught his eye, and I knew that he knew it. He never did it again and I think, after that, he began to enjoy my suggestions and the way I worked...

Frankly, when I hear people are difficult, I tend to think – good, that'll be challenging. They are bound to be something special. And there's no doubt at all that he was – absolutely uncompromising, uncomfortably so at times. But the production side saw the worst of that. He expected the time and money they gave him in Russia, and it just wasn't available...

[47] V. John, G. Petrie, *The Films of Andrei Tarkovsky,* Indiana University press, Bloomington and Indiana 1994, p.49
[48] Layla Garrett, *Independent,* October 17, 1993

*With some of the cast, it was different. Some of the Swedes found it a little
difficult because they were hesitant to tell him when things weren't right. I
had no such inhibitions after my training in the theatre, where so much is a
kind of co-operative venture.'* [49]

He wasn't always formidable. Susan also said that 'When I hear people say in
solemn tones, 'Oh, you worked with Andrei Tarkovsky', I remember this cheeky
little chappie who was doing the most outrageous things, pulling faces and
gambolling around'. [50]

Essentially, however, he was deeply, indeed tragically serious. Through him, the
Russian nineteenth century becomes immediately apparent, with Dostoevsky as
perhaps the most kindred spirit. Tarkovsky was spiritual and anti-materialistic,
which made him almost as critical of the West as of the East. He wrote that;

*'The artist is always a servant, and is perpetually trying to pay for the gift that
has been given to him as if by a miracle... Modern man, however, does not
want to make any sacrifice, even though true affirmation of self can only be
expressed in sacrifice.'* [51]

Deeper even than the German instinct to obey is the Russian instinct for self-
annihilation. Tarkovsky's hero in this film has begun the process before the action
begins, by abandoning his successful career as an actor. He meditates not
speaking any more, an idea he turns into a vow when he makes a bargain with
God, that if they are spared the horrors of nuclear war, which seems imminent,
he will also not see his son any more, and will burn down his house. He hates the
condition of 'animal fear' to which he has been reduced. He goes through with
this, but when they survive the night, and the world is spared, he seems in a state
of madness, as the house burns. He runs hither and thither in an exotic dressing
gown. There is none of the tranquillity of a man who is in touch with God. There
was no communication with the family about his decision. In a note on Hamlet,

[49] Derek Malcolm 'Tarkovsky's Other Woman', *Guardian*, June 9, 1987
[50] V. John, G. Petrie, op. cit. p.41
[51] A. Tarkovsky, *Sculpting in Time: Reflections on the Cinema*, translated Kitty Hunter-Blair, Faber and Faber
1989 p.38

the work he was to film next, had he survived, Tarkovsky wrote that 'This desire to suffer without any organized religious system can become simply psychotic.'[52] This looks like what happens here. There is an alternative story, almost, in his encounter with Maria, an attractive young witch, during the long night before the decisive dawn. The philosophic postman, Otto, urged him to sleep with her, to save the world. He does so, albeit with very little confidence or enjoyment, and they make love in a state of levitation. One might take the view that, given the imminence of Armageddon, Alexander is actually having a rattling good time, retiring from his responsibilities, after all this fun, in an ambulance.

Reviews and critical studies were solemn and appreciative, but doubtful. It won the Special Jury Prize at Cannes in 1986, but the *Sunday Times* reviewer noted that lots of people didn't stay until the end of the viewing. 'We must confront the glittering eye of this ancient mariner calling us to our spiritual duties', wrote Philip French.[53] 'He stands for something we are in need of', wrote Mark le Fanu, 'even if we can't name it precisely'.[54]

The full burden of pain and incomprehension is felt by the hero's wife, Adelaide (Susan), who feels betrayed by his retreat from the theatre. When news of the coming war breaks, she has all the 'animal fear' her husband loathes. She throws a fit. Susan recalled:

> *'I remember very clearly what happened when I had to do my hysterical scene. He seemed to expect me simply to turn it on when the time was ripe. So I said to him: It's going to be no good if you just shout 'action'. Can I actually do the action bit myself? He was very doubtful. But I said it would only take half a minute for me to get in the right frame of mind, and that I'd bang on the floor when I was ready. He looked puzzled, but he let me do it, and I must say he seemed quite mesmerised by the result.'* [55]

[52] A. Tarkovsky, *Time within Time: The Diaries 1970-1986* translated Kitty Hunter-Blair, Faber and Faber 1994, p.378
[53] Philip French, *Observer*, January 11, 1987
[54] Mark le Fanu, *Sight and Sound*, Autumn 1986
[55] Derek Malcolm, op. cit.

Any less response would have been surprising, for this is one of the most extraordinary pieces of acting I have ever seen. These are not picturesque hysterics, but a raw, ugly, terrifying ordeal, as though hideous bolts of alien energy were coming into her body from the air; and it lasts. Her husband leaves others to comfort her. When she recovers, she says that she has not known love, having fought something inside herself in her marriage, and raged at her husband for not being what she wants. Given his self-absorption, this seems comprehensible. There is a hint that she may be having an affair with Viktor, the family doctor.

Mark le Fanu calls her 'surely the least sympathetic of all Tarkovsky's women characters',[56] and Tarkovsky himself wrote of her in his *Sculpting in Time* as a monster of egotism. He told Susan that the character 'was absolutely run by her emotional life. So I asked him whether she was not pretty selfish, and he roared with laughter. Well, that's what I thought. Selfish to the point of being comic. And in a sense, that's how I played her.'[57] There is hardly a trace of comedy in the film but there is a humanity to Adelaide. When the maid refused to wake up Little Man, as she had commanded, she accepts the decision quite meekly.

When Sue met Tarkovsky's wife Larissa, she realised how close the character of Adelaide was to her. 'This isn't to say that the two are the same … But there are clear parallels and had I seen Larissa beforehand, I wouldn't have had to ask those questions at all.'[58] When she came to portray Chekhov's Anna Arkedina, Susan drew on Larissa. 'The whole of her face quivered with emotion … She would come in with a letter suddenly, tears pouring down her face. The next moment she would call "Caviar, caviar!" It was absolutely exhausting'.[59] Susan's mother recalls Susan saying that Larissa terrified everyone on the set. It makes us wonder anew if Dostoevsky's characters aren't simply true.

Susan found her character at least partly exhilarating, calling her 'destructive, but capable of enormous warmth and love'. There is a tremendous pent-up energy in

---

[56] Mark le Fanu, *Cinema of Andrei Tarkovsky*, BFI 1987, p.128
[57] Derek Malcolm, op. cit.
[58] Derek Malcolm, op. cit.
[59] Vera Lustig, *Plays and Players*, February 1991

her, which could come out as a terrible rage against the world, quite different from the icy calm that Alexander aspires to. Layla Garrett recalls that 'Andrei called Susan "our intellectual". He was fascinated and at the same time unsettled by her directness and insatiable curiosity. "Susan's going to corner me again", he'd say, tugging on his moustache.'[60] She went in some awe of him, however:

> '*He talked about faith and how hard it was. And he talked about it with such purity that it was intensely moving … That day, I saw such compassion in the man and such feeling that all I could do was to thank my lucky stars that I had the chance to share the experience with him of making the film.*'[61]

She took the Russian promise of spirituality and excitement completely seriously. She longed, she said, to meet a Russian man who would sweep her off her feet. All her men to date had been frightened of her. Imaginatively and creatively, Tarkovsky was the man, and some of her deep power had been unleashed in Adelaide. It was to be a unique experience, however; at the end of 1985 Tarkosvky was diagnosed as having lung cancer. He died on December 29th 1986, in Paris.

It is probable that they would have made many more films together and impossible to say where that would have led her as an actress. In *The Sacrifice* we usually see her in long shots against a bleak landscape and hear her voice only in fragments. Two other actresses were used to supply the rest of her dialogue, as she hadn't had time to learn Swedish. Her dress and hairstyle look archaic, Chekhovian; it is a film of quite daunting austerity. If this is a pinnacle of her career, it is a very isolated pinnacle, shrouded in mist. I feel Tarkovsky might have made her into another Liv Ullman, all soul and tragic intensity.

In the same year Tarkovsky died, when Susan was working in London's familiar West End again, alongside Paul Scofield in the comedy *I'm not Rappaport*, her dresser felt lumps in her body; they would be diagnosed as cancerous…

[60] Layla Garrett, op. cit.
[61] Derek Malcolm, op. cit.

Part Four (1986-1995):

But What About Me?

VII.   Theatre, Radio, Film & Television 1986-1995

SUSAN'S STRATEGY FOR DEALING WITH HER ILLNESS was to keep it a secret from all but her family and a few friends, such as Sister Olive and Rosemary Marter. Rosemary was an old schoolfriend who had worked her way through acting to psychotherapy. They had kept in touch and there was a closeness that Susan could draw on. Very few were so privileged. In showbiz, if you are known to be ill, you get no work. Acting was not only her sole source of income; it was her life. Unemployment would mean low morale, which would lessen her chances of recovery. Mercifully, she was spared that ordeal, and the amount of work she got through in these last nine years was phenomenal.

The actual treatment was to be, at first, alternative rather than surgical, with a strict macrobiotic diet and lots of exercise. As Terry Hands put it, she took to 'living in a plastic bag'. As her new habits could not be invisible, she passed them off as personal eccentricities. On the set of *White Mischief*, Charles Dance recalls her clanking up to her room with a collection of pots and pans and woks to do her own cooking; strange smells would issue forth. She rarely, if ever, ate with the rest of the cast. When she went to restaurants with groups, she would order plain boiled rice and even provide her own teabags, although she insisted on paying a full share of the bill. On the set of *The Seagull* her birthday came up and the best present the cast could think of was edible seaweed. She laughed and joked about all this and spoke of food allergies, but nobody guessed there was something more serious afoot.

For her career, she thought she would ease up on stage appearances, which are enormously demanding of energy, and concentrate on film and television, to establish her reputation, bring in some more serious money, and enable her to make a triumphant return to the stage, energy and health restored. Up to a point, it worked.

In 1986, when she discovered her condition, she was making her first appearance in the West End in *I'm not Rappaport*. She was Clara, daughter to her old Jewish father Nat (Paul Scofield), a proud socialist agitator of 1909 vintage. All through college years she was his disciple. 'I was the only kid on the Columbia riot whose father showed up to coach! I still don't believe it!' Now she has gone in for business, marriage and children who believe profoundly in cable TV, as Nat puts it. She laughs sadly and sympathetically at the beliefs they used to share, but she wants to stop him eternally getting into trouble, with close supervision. To this he finally has to bow. Susan believed that 'Sco' approached the part as earnestly as he did Oberon:

> 'You can see his art at work. He thinks a lot at home. He doesn't do a great deal of discussing. He comes into rehearsals with private things he has worked out which he reveals only slowly. It's quite a private process. It's a huge part for him. In the early days there was quite a panic. It was slow going. Then once we were working without the script he really opened up and charged through it. It was marvellous to watch him … He does have something secret about him. There is a quality of mystery which some women have but very few men. It is something you never quite get to the heart of.' [1]

The last lines apply equally well to her. Paul Scofield thought very highly of Susan. 'I loved Susan so much and my memories of her are so sharp … her courage and sweetness and lightness of touch in rehearsal and performance gave the lie to what must have been her fears. To us who worked with her there was no sign of anxiety. I noticed that when she had the opportunity she would lie down in her darkened dressing room for half an hour or so, and we all knew, or felt, that this was necessary to her, and she was seldom disturbed.' [2] She was sociable when Julian Curry and Norman Rodway came to see her in her dressing room. They drank wine and talked for so long they didn't notice that everybody else had locked up and gone home. They had to climb out of the Apollo Theatre by the scaffolding.

The play was called sentimental and 'artful' by several critics. Susan drew some rare praise from Milton Shulman for 'a sympathetic impression of a daughter

---

[1] *Evening Standard* 4.7.86
[2] Paul Scofield, letter to author 5.11.99

hearing for the thousandth time the same arguments and jokes'.[3] Michael Billington thought that she 'lent Nat's daughter a genuine sense of filial frustration and concern'. He added, in parenthesis, 'why is she not playing major roles?'[4] He had seen her often enough in major Shakespearean roles, so he must have been referring to other contexts. She was not destined to go much further in the West End, and that caused her no special regret.

There was just one more foray in that direction with her appearance in Pinero's *The Cabinet Minister*, at the Royal Exchange Manchester in 1988. The play was getting its first major revival since Pinero had launched it as a farce in the 1890s. Critics find it hard to classify as a piece – too substantial and serious for a farce, but not so definite as Wildean or Shavian drama. The director, Braham Murray, said that, being Jewish himself, he understood Pinero's position as a Jew back then, looking at the English aristocracy from the outside. The rather thin plot concerns husband-hunting, blackmail, debts, government secrets and insider deals. Susan played Lady Kitty Twombley, wife to Sir Julian Twombley. She dreads a return to the countryside (whence she came) and its economical ways, but that fate looms for her at the end, after she has got her daughter married, and narrowly avoided a scandal. Sue's dialogue is as skittish and self-centred as everybody else's.

Braham Murray thought she came to the part quite easily. She became anxious about getting no notes from him during rehearsals. She didn't need them. It was perhaps the undemanding nature of the part that worried her. According to Michael Ratcliffe, however, she played the part 'with single-minded energy and zeal',[5] and Randal Herley, who played the servant, Probyn, thought that she 'filled the stage with warmth and energy and glamour'. He saw a Celtic quality in her:

'I was aware of a small questioning smile which lurked strangely vulnerably, in eyes which gazed firmly at one in an often serious – even severe – face. It

---

[3] Milton Shulman, *Evening Standard* 4.7.86
[4] Michael Billington, *Guardian*, 4.7.86
[5] Michael Ratcliffe, *Observer*, 3.1.88

*was those dark eyes and the body language, suggesting a capacity for fierce
and passionate feelings, that seemed to hint at dark Celt blood.*[6]

A few years later the play went to London's West End and Braham Murray wrote
to Susan apologising for the fact that Derek Nimmo and Maureen Lipmann were
to appear as the MP and his wife. Susan said she quite understood West End
criteria and, with no disrespect to those actors, wasn't too upset about it.

The one major play she undertook before her return to the RSC was Strindberg's
The Father, which David Leveaux directed at the National in October 1988. Sue
was Laura to Alun Armstrong's Captain. She told Dominic Gray, in a tone of
regret, 'I can't resist the theatre. I keep being offered these wonderful parts'. She
had a sense that her power was under-used. 'I've always felt slightly out of place
here, I feel myself more European, more emotional, stronger and more
committed than a lot of people think an actor should be; things which are
frowned on here.' Working on *The Father* was a joy, but also 'like going through
open-heart surgery every day ... thrilling and really upsetting' at the same time.[7]
She liked the gritty quality of John Osborne's adaptation; for instance, at the end
of the first act:

> *Laura: What if I were just telling the truth when I said Bertha was my child
> and not yours? Suppose...*
> *Captain: Stop it!*
> *Laura: Bite on that ! Where would your rights be then?*[8]

Peter Watts' Penguin translation of 1955 just has 'Suppose it were true, you'd
have no more rights.'

Laura can be played for straight aggression, cunning and with a will of iron as she
campaigns to get her husband committed so that she can control the destiny of
the daughter. Susan played her as 'a richly expressive departure from stereotype',[9]
'...ashen faced, eyes staring, body rigidly angular, as though she herself were on

---

[6] Randal Herley, letter to author 5.8.98
[7] Dominic Gray, 'A Fleeting Glimpse', *What's On*, October 1988
[8] John Osborne, *The Father and Hedda Gabler*, Faber and Faber 1989, p.20
[9] Irving Wardle, *The Times*, 27.10.88

the verge of madness. When she laughs, it is the hysterical laughter of someone about to burst into tears. In her titanic struggle with her husband, she suffers moments of numbing weakness. I have never seen the role played in precisely this manner. I have rarely seen it played better'.[10]

David Benedictine said, 'Susan Fleetwood is the best actress in the country for exciting our pity and terror. As soon as she comes on, you know, your heart goes out to her.' [11] 'Susan Fleetwood finds extraordinary emotional variety in the role. At first she is all melting, wasp-waisted deference. Later she hits a vein of sardonic comedy when, having destroyed her husband by querying his paternity, she delicately enquires, "There's nothing wrong, is there?" And at the climax she hints that there is something echoingly hollow in her moment of spectacular triumph'.[12]

Michael Ratcliffe thought that 'her meekness in victory is appalling'.[13]

'In her superbly disquieting performance... there is a mad, unfixed quality to Fleetwood's eyes which suggests both conscious evil and that she is being swept forward by an instinct over which she has little control.' [14]

Annie Smart's design was almost Gothic expressionism. 'Colour contrasts are excellently used so that the captain inhabits an ashen study while Laura constantly emerges from a sloping, blood-red dining-room like a vengeful Clytemnestra (even her bottle-green dress opens out to reveal a scarlet lining).' [15] Antonia Byatt thought that she 'moved like a snake in this green dress'.[16] The reading seems faithful to the text. The captain's criticism of the women who over-populate the house is that they lack common sense, are in fact crazy – artistically, religiously, morally. Laura can't even spot a lodger who won't pay. Their religion exempts them from having any morals. Laura has no rational plan for her

[10] Francis King, *Sunday Telegraph*, 30.10.88
[11] David Benedict 'Kaleidescope' BBC Radio 4, 4.10.88. Script in Royal National Theatre Archives.
[12] Michael Billington, *Guardian* 28.10.88
[13] Michael Ratcliffe, *Observer* 6.11.88
[14] Paul Taylor, *Independent* 29.10.88
[15] Michael Billington, *Guardian* 28.10.88
[16] Antonia Byatt, 'Kaleidescope' Radio 4; 27.10.88

daughter's future, she merely projects a fantasy of her own, in an emanation of power.

Susan never played any role for unmixed aggression. With simpler parts, she fused grief and anger. One such came in 'The Leper of St. Giles' – an episode of the TV series '*Cadfael*' in 1994 (with Derek Jacobi as the priestly sleuth). She played a shrewish noblewoman, Lady Anne Picard, who along with her villainous husband Godfrey (Jonathan Hyde) wants to marry off her niece for the usual mercenary reasons. According to Sara Badel, some of the younger actors on the set were taking life a bit easy. 'Watch Sue,' Derek Jacobi told her, 'she'll show them how it's done'.[17] She has two fine moments of acting outside the stereotype. She collapses in grief, mouth wide open in soundless crying, on hearing that her husband has been killed. Later, when the killer is unmasked, she storms down the priory steps towards him like a colourful avalanche, and looks ready to strangle him before she is dragged off.

Her purest portrait in this vein had come in 1992, when her old friend Bill Bryden directed her in a black and white TV version of *Six Characters in Search of an Author*. She had lost none of her satirical edge. When the new BBC personal assistant came in, Susan shook her head and said quietly 'Not for Billy!' She was also amused to find that the part consisted largely of weeping. She played the mother, whose aim in life is to keep alive her grief and fury at her husband's doings regarding their daughter. No change or development is allowed for in the writing, but she comes across as neither risible nor monstrous. Her most touching moment comes when, her bewildered white face staring from her black widow's weeds, she says of her husband (John Hurt), 'you're good at talking. I'm not. But, believe me, when he married me, though goodness knows why he did, I was always a simple person, no money or anything…' She is also capable of a fury that has her lunging at Madam Pace – played by Patricia Hayes as a highly indignant eccentric.

In the same year as *The Father* (1988) she appeared in Alan Wymark's *Strike up the Banns*, a suburban comedy directed by another old friend, Richard Cottrell,

---

[17] Sara Badel, phone interview, 21.10.99

at the Theatr Clwyd. She played Geraldine, a housewife so oppressed by propriety that she disguises herself as a fictitious brother Robb, who is not only a cad but a bounder too (the distinction is unclear to me); this disrupts an important dinner party. The rebellion is limited, and there is a happy ending. It is another example, as in 1971, of her playing a strongly tragic role and a completely light-hearted one in the same period. The play had quite a short run.

Susan did make a triumphal return to the stage at Stratford in 1990. 'Stratford itself I could do without' she said, 'I always feel like Big Ears in Noddy'. It had become something of a tourist theme park. For the theatre people there, of course, she had warm feelings. It hadn't changed all that much, she thought, from the days of Peter Hall. There was still more of a family feeling up there than in London, where everyone scattered after a performance. Her dressing room had a French window which overlooked the river, whereas in the Barbican she was, like everyone else, away from natural light.

The training of young actors, she thought, had changed. 'The emphasis is not on doing Shakespeare, as it was in my day.'[18] She, however, was to play Beatrice, a role she had looked forward to from 1982, and Anna Arkadina in *The Seagull*. Terry Hands was to retire as director in July 1991, handing over to Adrian Noble, so this was the last season there for both of them. 'I am here this season to salute Terry. Absolutely. He has absolutely dedicated his life to theatre and the RSC and has done some really fine work'.[19] '...I've worked a lot with Terry Hands at Liverpool and at the Aldwych, so that we have a formula; it's comforting that he knows what I'm capable of doing. When you're working with a new director there's the feeling, "Oh dear, he's got to get used to me". Basically I like directors who find the people they're working with attractive, because I think there's got to be a kind of relationship between the actors and the director which is almost sexual – by that I don't mean sexy – a sort of bond-feeling.'[20]

She had one well-deserved moment. 'I walked into the middle of the stage and it was difficult to believe I had been away all that time. Then I heard this wonderful

---

[18] Jeremy Herbert, *Stratford Herald* 20.4.90
[19] *Leicester Mercury* 6.4.90
[20] Vera Lustig, 'Diva', *Plays and Players* Feb. 1991

chorus "Hello, Sue, nice to see you," like I had only been away for five minutes. Some of the chaps in the props and the costume department up in Stratford I have known for the past twenty years'.[21] God knows what all her thoughts were. She must have recalled old times with Terry when they had both swept into the place back in 1966. She would not make another comeback; she was by now seriously ill. Just four weeks before going on as Beatrice she had had a mastectomy, but still very few knew that anything was wrong...

She had time to notch up some tremendous acting successes still. She thought she had played almost every kind of woman. 'I like bouncing on that kind of tightrope ... I think that's something I go towards because I think I have a strong spirit – but perhaps I make some more spirited than they might have been.' Beatrice she thought 'delicious ... a wonderful, eruptive person, an oddball, like Benedict. The two don't fit into their society. Beatrice is quick, sharp, vulnerable, then there are moments when she is pure joy, when she wants to just fly for the hell of it. She resembles Arkadina, for both are vital characters, both wicked in their different ways ... They are both very sexy, and that is fine. Not every part allows that fruitiness – so there's a lot of wiggling to do, a lot of sauce to be relished in both of them ... I've never worked with Roger before. But we'll buzz one another up and be a treat, playing comedy and tragedy'. Her Benedict was Roger Allam, and the chemistry between them was all she expected, and more. 'I could tell almost instantly we'd get on ... we've been absolutely diabolical to each other in rehearsal'.[22]

She was living the part; there was a streak of buried aggression in Susan that surfaced with Beatrice:

> 'There is quite a lot of Beatrice in me. It is quite dangerous. I'm beginning to be quite sharp with people and I am playing tricks on them. In a supermarket the other day I found myself saying to the people around me "Well, be happy with your boring little lives then". Before then I had just thought it'.[23]

---

[21] Jeremy Herbert, op. cit.
[22] S. Barker, *Solihull News* 14.6.90
[23] Jeremy Herbert, op. cit.

It went further than that. Once a young actress was drifting about at the morning rehearsal, having made a night of it, rambling on, with a beer can in one hand and a cigarette in the other. Sue removed the can and the fag and hit her. 'Show up for the matinee!' She did. Susan had no time to waste.

The reviews were mostly very favourable:

> 'a high-octane treat from Susan Fleetwood, who bounces her sharp exchanges across the stage with maximum glee'.[24]

> 'As Amazons go she is kind and humorous but formidable'.[25]

> 'Beatrice is Susan Fleetwood, here playing not for laughs but for remorse and concern as she swallows the bait about Benedict's alleged love for her. Miss Fleetwood is a ridiculously underused actress. This Beatrice can touch the heart with "My mother cried; but then there was a star danced and under that I was born." Her rage at her cousin's betrayal is furious and frightening. And the scene of cautious admission of love between her and Benedict, old sparring partners incredulously drawn towards each other, was played, tearful and tense, to a breathless silent house.'[26]

Michael Billington thought it not a match made in heaven and that Beatrice the lover and the avenger were not reconciled. I saw it and have brushed up my memory with an RSC tape and see no such problem. As when I saw Judi Dench play Lady Macbeth, I felt that I couldn't believe that any other actress I had ever seen could bring off the part so well. This was a warm-hearted, impulsive Beatrice, flourishing a rapier in the opening scene as though she knew how to use it, holding it horizontally above her head after the first exchange with Benedict and flinging down a glove, as though inviting him to come on and do better. Just once Sue was making a mess of the swordplay. Paul Webster, playing Leonato, asked her if something was wrong. She burst into tears, saying that she had accidentally read a hostile review in some incidental Stratford paper. Usually

---

[24] John Marrick, *Daily Mail* 11.4.90
[25] Benedict Nightingale, *The Times* 11.4.90
[26] Martin Hoyle, *Financial Times* 12.4.90

she didn't read critics at all. 'Silly fuckers,' she called them. Her fragile confidence was momentarily shattered. It came back, and she radiated the pleasure she took in her part.[27]

All her fun comes out when she speaks of leading apes in hell (apes, like virgins, being a useless breed), and she briefly adopts the voice of a crabby old man, as the devil, in 'get you to heaven, Beatrice'. She spends much of that scene on a swing, but jumps down to demonstrate the Scotch jig. She overhears all of Benedict saying he can take no more of her, which paves the way for the soliloquy, "What fire is in mine ears..." in which 'she flattens herself against the wall and listens in appalled recognition as Hero and Margaret take her character to pieces'.[28]

She made the best of this beautiful speech, beginning softly with just a touch of tears, but sounding 'Contempt farewell...' loudly. 'Others say thou dost deserve' had the old arch tone of wit, but 'I'll believe it' felt like the acceptance of a miracle. Her anger with Claudio was formidable. 'But manhood is melted into curtsies' was slow and heavy, then the pace quickened with the rise of her temper. It is a rich, noble anger on behalf of someone else. She would be a wonderful friend, and a bad enemy to the enemies of her friends. She told Paul Webster she could not have played that scene so well had he not been such a good Leonato; he was glad to hear it.

The part demands tremendous energy and vivacity. At the end she is dancing, shaking her mane of hair in exuberance, with a gravelly tone to her voice, relishing the triumph of how things have turned out. When she was not on stage, she was in bed, recuperating. Her mother had rented accommodation near Stratford, and tended to Susan, to get her through what she had to do.

After this, Chekhov was a holiday, she said. She relished returning to him, sending little cards to Amanda Root (Nina) with seagulls on them and the inscription 'Aren't we lucky?' 'In Chekhov there seems to be a more equal division between the action, the feeling and the talking, whereas in Shakespeare

---

[27] Paul Webster, letter to author, 12.3.98
[28] Irving Wardle, *Independent on Sunday*, 15.4.90

everything that you feel has to be expressed in words'. Her preparations were no less thorough than usual. So good were her notes that other people's notes were based upon them. Terry Hands, directing, let everyone have more freedom than usual until the last two weeks of rehearsal, when they were all drawn in together.

'We all very much felt that we'd written our version of the play.' The actors realised that Terry had slyly cast them according to type. Anna Arkadina, actress and mother, was a challenge. 'Normally I will try to get into the mood of the scenes, but with Arkadina that's impossible. She'll come in one state of mind and then within ten seconds that will have changed.' Susan came to like this, as she grew into the part. 'I like to make infinitesimal changes from one night to another. Some actors find this disconcerting, and think something's gone wrong, but I just like to throw it around a bit... But that's why I enjoy working with Simon (Russell Beale) because he will respond to those changes.' Anna she both liked and disliked. 'There are parts of her I dislike intensely – her terrible selfishness, the way she treats poor Konstantin and Nina. But she does live life in spades. She goes for it. And she's good value... Anna's great to have around, but she's a disaster on legs.'[29] Memories of Tarkovsky's wife helped.

Most reviews thought that Anna's self-absorption had been admirably caught: 'almost tipsy on her own vulgar self-obsession';[30] 'gazing distractedly into imaginary mirrors';[31] 'a riveting portrait of self-admiring actressy insensitivity'.[32] 'Her manipulative *volte-faces* were particularly impressive ... if you had to be adopted by either actress, you'd choose Joan Crawford';[33]

> *'... a ripe, posing, highly sexed Arkadina, every inch the spoilt diva.*
> *Shamelessly she parades her neatly clinched waist in its cascade of cream*
> *lace, her face crumpling into tears when thwarted, her hands groping through*
> *the air as though searching for the perfect gesture – or perhaps for something*
> *missing from her pampered, vapid existence. The voice caresses Amanda*

[29] Vera Lustig, 'Diva', *Plays and Players*, February 1991
[30] *Time Out*, 10.7.91
[31] Michael Billington, *Guardian*, 13.7.91
[32] John Peters, *Sunday Times*, 11.11.91
[33] Paul Taylor, *Independent*, 8.11.91

> *Root's gauche, dowdy Nina with the gracious condescension of someone*
> *heedless of the damage they're inflicting. In short, it's a magnificent*
> *performance, teetering bravely on the brink of parody, very much what you*
> *would expect from the actor who gave us a terrifying obsessive Laura in the*
> *National's* The Father *two years ago. Yet it fits in seamlessly with the rest of*
> *Terry Hands's superb production, 'so robust' as Fleetwood herself says*
> *approvingly of the ensemble result.'* [34]

Anna calls for a virtuoso player. Charles Dance said that Susan was the only actress he knew who could make an entrance backwards, on an intake of breath, to the sound of raucous laughter in the wings. Amanda Root admired her energy. 'She was out there, she was fighting'. Anna does have a human side. As the photographs show, Susan was beautiful enough to deliver some lines with great conviction. 'I'm always properly dressed and have my hair done just *comme il faut* … There! you see! I'm as spry as a kitten …'

Despite this, there is more than a touch of jealously in her reactions to Nina, who has her life still ahead of her. Also, Konstantin (Simon Russell Beale) does attack her acting, and she is bound to resent this. She repents lyrically, but momentarily. 'Forgive your wicked mother. Forgive an unhappy woman.' She has very little reaction to his first shooting of himself. She hero-worships Trigorin, but not as Nina does. One does not envy him as the man to whom she goes down on her knees, rabidly urging him not to go, then telling him, almost conspiratorially, 'you're the only hope of Russia'. The *Times* reviewer noticed that 'half way through this outburst of furious talk a change in tone comes into her voice, faint but definite. She is expressing the pain of a woman whose lover may be leaving her, but the artist in her, the actress, is feeling its way forward again. Like Roger Allam's mellifluous Trigorin, setting down little phrases for his stories, she is noticing the sound of her rage.'[35] She, like Trigorin, is much absorbed in her art, and needs an audience, but not intimates. She does not know herself when she is genuine and when she is fake.

---

[34] Vera Lustig, op. cit.
[35] Jeremy Kingston, *The Times*, 12.7.91

Susan's last stage appearance was as Ellen in Robin Lefevre's production of Sam Shepard's *Curse of the Starving Class*, in September 1991. She had been out to California to see brother Mick and to study the local accent, since it is set in the California desert. It is a very pronounced accent and one presumes that she got it right. The play was not very widely reviewed, as *Measure for Measure* at the Other Place and *Liaisons Dangereuses* took up lots of space.

As Ella, Susan whined and roared very authentically in the manner of an American lady of a certain age who isn't getting her way. Nobody gets their way, in this highly dysfunctional family. Whoever is the rightful owner of the place, none of *them* are, and men come to blow up the car, which hasn't been paid for. The daughter takes off for a life of crime. There is the one moment of tragic intensity at the end when Ella and her son Wesley share a memory of an eagle swooping on a cat, and find an image that sums up their family. 'And they fight. They fight like crazy in the middle of the sky. The cat's tearing his chest out, and the eagle's trying to drop him, but the cat won't let go because he knows if he falls he'll die. And they come crashing down to the earth. Both of them come crashing down like one whole thing.' Susan delivered this in a huge, musical, impassioned voice.

In quality, after Anna Arkadina, Susan's great triumph with natural-born actresses was Eva Kay, in *The Buddha of Suburbia*, a four-part television version of the Hanif Kureishi novel of 1990. Roger Michell did the screenplay and the directing. He said that Susan was thrilled to get the part. She went off to Covent Garden to buy some designer clothes, a luxury she rarely allowed herself. She had as much fun with the part as if it had been her first school play. Working on it with her, Brenda Blethyn recalled, 'There was always a lot of hilarity. That's what I remember most. And for some reason she liked to kick me up the bum! Repeatedly. Probably because my bum was just about level with her knee! She was upwards of 5 feet 10 inches tall and I'm only five feet two inches. We developed a special bum-kicking dance. Susan and I didn't ever do anything really intellectual together, we were just extremely silly, joking and laughing and being totally absurd. It was impossible for us to be sensible together – even after she became ill.'[36]

Sue plays a divorced mother, an enthusiastic latter-day hippy, 'all henna, joss sticks and scarves' as the *Times* reviewer put it.[37] The young hero, Karim, describes her in the book as very open about her feelings, always passionate about something and with all her life available to her at once, 'as if she could move from age to age according to how she felt'. She takes up with Karim's father, Haroon Anwar (Roshan Seth), an Asian Mr Chadband, who makes a good living enunciating Eastern platitudes at trendy gatherings.

There is an hilarious moment early on at one such, when they are all sitting in a circle, and all have to throw up their arms and stick their tongues out, 'getting in touch with my feelings, and all that crap' in the immortal words of Annie Hall. Eva tells young Karim that 'the beautiful should get everything they want', and that the ugly 'are to be blamed, not pitied'. She justifiably counts herself among the beautiful. The ugly are represented by Changez, a well-born but unattractive, indeed deformed Indian who comes to fulfil an arranged marriage, and falls in love with his wife, only to find that she'll sleep with many people of both sexes, only not him.

There is a hard streak in Eva that she shares with her frightening son Charlie (Steve Mackintosh), hell-bent on success as a punk rocker. He has a permanent, hard *Clockwork Orange* stare. Success doesn't take long, but before he gets it he steals her paintings to pay for his drugs. She won't admit anything wrong. 'Genet was a thief, wasn't he?' She weeps when he takes to wearing a swastika, crying 'Where's the compassion?'- but when she goes to a punk rock gig with people screaming and leaping about, bottles flying and blood flowing, a look of awe and laughter comes over her. It is excitement; it is what she wants.

Back at home, her meditations take a practical turn. 'I've made my choice… white is the only colour for a house'. She gets Karim's uncle Ted (John McEnery) to do up her house, not telling him it's to sell, to get into London. She leads them

---

[36] Brenda Blethyn, letter to author 8.12.99
[37] L. Tron, *The Times*, 4.11.93

all round the room on a serpentine dance, like a Pied Piper, chanting the names of London streets and shops, and it works, they all follow; 'White 'Art Lane' is uncle Ted's contribution. She promotes Karim's career and Haroon's by giving parties to which she invites all the right people. At the end she marries Haroon and turns into a Thatcherite just as that lady enters history with her election victory of 1979. It is the least sympathetic part Susan ever undertook, but done with great panache.

Susan was now back in Greenwood Rd, Hackney, alone. Anxious to keep busy and to make money, of which she was short, she undertook a lot of television work. Much of it was routine: a *Bill* episode, a *Minder*, an *Under the Hammer*, and a part in a bizarre play by Andrew Davies – *A Few Short Journeys of the Heart*.

Flying in the Branches was a mildly interesting play of January 1989. Susan plays a Czech lady married to an Englishman. She liked playing a mid-European. 'I very much respond to their emotional honesty and their sensitivity. I just love being around them … it's been a most stimulating experience'.[38] She puts on a headscarf at the end, and with her dark, intense eyes, suddenly looks completely foreign. Her pretty sister Dana (Edita Brychta) comes on a ten-day visit, desperate to find a husband to get her out of Czechoslovakia. Susan (Susanna in the story) is very critical. 'It's immoral,' she cries, her voice assuming its native accent, as happens when people lose their tempers.

In the same year she appeared alongside Sir John Gielgud in a four-part adaptation of John Mortimer's novel *Summer's Lease*. She was Molly Pargeter, daughter to Haverford Downs, an elegant essayist of the old school, and a *roué*. His conversation is appallingly salacious, which amuses the children but distresses Molly's proper solicitor husband Hugh (Michael Pennington). Haverford loves all things Italian, of course, and is genuinely adventurous. He talks his way into an apartment with a view of the Palio horse race in Siena, with all the family. He throws himself unsuccessfully at an old flame (he says; she can't remember). He is not there just for laughs. He understands Molly pretty well. They are joined, he says, by a 'sneaking respect for excess'.

---

[38] *Radio Times*, 22.1.89, p.22

Molly finds out that Hugh has been meeting one of his lady clients rather often, but is disgusted to find that it hasn't even been an affair. 'You're so English. You haven't even the courage to screw her!' Would she prefer the Italian way of nursing jealousy to the point of murder (the upshot of the plot)? No. She makes up with Hugh before they get home, and there is some very vigorous lovemaking.

'The whole production was a very happy experience,' she said. 'When John Mortimer asked me, rather nervously, what I thought of Molly, I was glad to be able to tell him I liked her. Of course, I've been able to fill in the bits he left out.'

'Because Molly isn't beautiful,' Mortimer said, 'I wanted a beautiful actress to play her and an actress moreover with a sense of humour'.

She was thrilled, of course, to be working alongside Sir John Gielgud. 'Sir John's going to steal the show,' she said (without a trace of rancour). 'It's such an outrageous part'. She found him 'a very funny man. Filled with life, wonderful entertainment value and quite incredible for his age ... He never stopped smoking and talking.' [39]

Filming was hot and tiring, and Sir John was unwell. He remembered Susan well 'as a charming colleague, kind and helpful ... I shall always remember her with the greatest pleasure and affection ... to salute her acting skill and personal charm ... both as an actress and comradeship at a particularly difficult time for me'. [40]

At this stage Susan still looked the picture of health, a huge mane of hair, good colour, and suggesting huge reserves of energy. Her fury at her husband is awesome. It is good to see her in full sunshine, in different costumes and glamorous settings like Siena. The series was well reviewed, but it couldn't bridge the gap between Chaintishire and the viewers Americans refer to as 'Joe Sixpack'; in England, the Royle family.

---

[39] Eithne Power, 'Chiantishire Downs', *Radio Times*, 28.10-Nov.3.11.89 pp. 4-5 John Mortimer's words quoted by Julie Allan.
[40] John Gielgud, letter to Bridget Fleetwood, 12.4.99

After shooting was over, her mother came out to join her, and they did the della Francesca trail together. Then they went to Venice, where Bridget suggested a gondola ride. 'No, we can't,' Susan said, 'we haven't got any lovers'.

An amateur detective here, she turned professional in her part in *Chandler and Co* (1995). She partners Ellie Chandler (Catherine Russell) in a female detective agency. Some of the stories are good, especially those by Paula Milne, who devised the series, but it never got near *Cracker* as a crime series or *Minder* as a portrait of a same-sex friendship. Everyone is too busy jumping in and out of cars and answering their mobiles to develop a relationship, so the characters end up all feeling pretty lightweight.

Susan took as much trouble over her part as any other, but there wasn't much of a distance to go. Kate, she thought, 'very much gives life a go, has a unique angle on things, and is surprisingly accurate at times ... Also she has an easy way with people. She is not a power dreamer, a business type. People do not feel threatened by her, so they trust her... I'm quite ordered and tidy, and Kate isn't at all ... She doesn't dress at all like I do, but I did choose the colours of the clothes. I love warm, autumn colours. They suit me and I feel good in them. I have always been very involved in the look of the characters I play. Right from the kick-off, when I read a part I see colour, texture and shape. It worries me if I have the wrong coloured socks on, even if they are completely hidden under a pair of boots'.[41]

She got on splendidly with Catherine Russell. They both consulted Lily Grant, a real private eye, who said that female private eyes were usually 'middle-aged mothers and housewives – so we're not tainted by the seedier sides of things.' When they went out on dry-run investigations, Catherine said, 'Sue was wonderful. She had made up a plausible story about a children's party and a lost flat number. She would be brilliant as a private eye'.[42] (Sue demurred.)

She was invited back to Susan's caravan, which was full of fabrics of all the crimsons and purples that she was wearing, ornaments, and a sound system, to

---

[41] 'Weekly News', BBC Press Cuttings 5.8.95.
[42] 'Weekly News', BBC Press Cuttings 5.8.95.

which she danced gleefully around. She appeared to be having fun and rejoicing in her slim figure. It was like being sixteen again, she said. So thin was she that it bemused the costume department, who were always giving her baggy things to wear. 'If they wanted a great fat blobby actress, why didn't they hire one?' she yelled. She was also very pallid, with a slight greenish tinge from all the healthy food she was eating. Catherine did guess that there was something quite wrong with her. She asked her if it was cancer. Sue said she wouldn't say yes or no, to avoid burdening her with the knowledge, 'but put it this way, I'll be wearing a lot of headscarves from now on'.[43] Neither Catherine nor anybody else guessed quite how ill she was. She spoke airily of feeling quite glad that her diary wasn't solidly booked for the next five years. She sounded as though she had a future:

> 'I'm a free spirit now as when I first started out as an actress – very much more experienced, but hopefully just as free… I think I knew very well what it would be like to have a family but I chose not to. I've got loads of nieces and nephews and I've had a lot of involvement with children – but when I have to go, I can do… No children, no pets, nothing. Just me, what I do, and my passport. That's how I like it.' [44]

Anne Skinner, the producer, thinks that it was only illness that prevented Susan from taking on a second series, but her director friend Richard Cottrell believes she wasn't fully satisfied artistically with what they had done. Reviewers had mostly been kind, and at one point they had ten million viewers, but the average was below that for the first series. The BBC still came to Susan with enthusiasm, saying 'Good news, there's to be another series!' 'Oh no there isn't', she replied.[45]

Susan had by then wound up her film career with two roles that could hardly be more different. One was that of Gwladys, Lady Delamere, mayor of Nairobi in 1941. This was in *White Mischief* (1987), a study of the wealthy white colonials enjoying their decadence in Happy Valley, Kenya, between the wars. When the Second World War comes, they see no reason to change their lifestyle.

---

[43] Catherine Russell, phone interview 21.12.99 44. BBC Press Cuttings, op. cit.
[44] James Parker, *Sunday Times*, 12.4.87
[45] Richard Cottrell, interview 11.8.99

Director Michael Radford describes the film as a 'requiem for the sixties'. The set had 'the grace and wit that belongs only to those who feel totally at ease'.[46] Belief in such a circle as the supreme flowering of English culture keeps on reviving at different times and places. Cyril Connolly was both fascinated and repelled by this set, and his notes on them were developed into a book by James Fox, in similar vein, in 1982. The interest lies in the murder of the great Don Juan, Lord Erroll (Charles Dance), after he has begun an open and vigorous affair with Diana Caldwell (Greta Scacchi). The obvious suspect, Diana's husband, Sir Jocelyn Broughton (Joss Acland) was tried and acquitted, part of his defence being that he had agreed to his wife having affairs. In practice, he finds her impossible to live with afterwards and kills himself (a departure from history).

Critics found the focus uncertain. Was it a murder story or a love story? Just what was the interest of this group? *Les Regles du Jeu* and *La Dolce Vita* were spoken of as having a clearer point of view. The film had to be re-financed half way through, and fears developed that libel suits could be brought by some of the survivors of that period. 'White cowboy' Kenyans were to be met even in the late eighties. This led to cuts. It was to have been a good deal longer, with much more about their relationship to the war, and a deeper portrait of the set in general. Hugh Grant would have done more than just bid Diana farewell, and Sarah Miles, as Alice de Janze, a particularly unstable and formidable club lady, would have figured more. There was a scene where she arrives in Nairobi, quite as much the grande dame as Josh Broughton's new bride, and waves her hat to the crowd from her railway carriage. Lord Erroll enters, lifts her skirt, and has her from behind. 'I wanted that kept in', Sarah said, 'but madame wouldn't have it!' Chagrin indeed. She got on very well with Susan, as did Charles Dance, who said 'Like everybody else, I adored her'.[47] Joss Acland says that this was the most enjoyable of all his films.[48] Not knowing Susan, he had wondered whether she had a sense of humour. 'Just you wait!' said Charles, and Joss soon changed his mind.

---

[46] James Parker, *Sunday Times*, 12.4.87
[47] Charles Dance, phone interview 21.10.99
[48] Joss Acland, phone interview, 11.11.99

Susan's part was indeterminate. She is no more responsible than any of the others. She is seen entering a room where a naked lady is enquiring of a circle of men just who is going to fuck her; the partner is to be chosen by the movement of a feather. What looks like studied vagueness overcomes Susan's face, until one realises that she is stoned on something. She finds it all a great joke. We see her later bustling off to a council meeting and lounging on the racecourse with Josh. At the trial, she is reduced to tears in the witness box, struggling against them as a lady trained not to show the softer emotions in public. The point is that she was madly in love with Erroll. The film gives her hardly any time to establish that; she stands at a dance, looking very serious, in a gorgeous blue dress and a gardenia in her hair, as Erroll leaves with Diana. Some thought her crazy enough to have killed him, through jealousy. She turns against Josh afterwards, describing him as a 'horrible man'.

The book portrays her as 'the hardest' of the set, 'a formidable old dragon', 'dotty' and violently jealous of younger women.[49] She was to die of blood pressure problems two years later. Had Susan been able to explore her in these directions, she would have emerged as a lot less sympathetic, and more disturbed, than the comparable memsahib figure from *Heat and Dust*, whom she here comes to resemble. Greta Scacchi scoops up the richest man around in both films.

White Mischief has a cult status in America, but wasn't too popular in Britain, despite its star-studded cast.

The type portrayed here goes back to Alsion, of *Look Back in Anger*, and Everyman days, the proper middle-class English lady. Susan played variants on this for her radio work of the period – Andromache in *King Priam* (1988), wife to an Ulsterman with sinister connections in *Where the Boys Are* (1990), wife to Dreyfus in *Prisoner of Honour* (1994) and the Madre of a convent in *Daughters of Venice* (1994).

The other film of her last period had one of her most remarkable roles ever, Aunt Rose in Peter Medak's film *The Krays* (1990). The film, shot in six weeks, was not

---

[49] James Fox, *White Mischief*, Jonathan Cape 1982, pp. 163-4

meant to be a deeply philosophic enquiry; it was meant to create a criminal world, like that of *The Godfather*. Charlie Kray and some broken-nosed, razor-scarred associates came along to lunch, and to advise on authenticity. Gary and Martin Kemp, of the pop group Spandau Ballet, play the twins. Through Mick, Susan knew enough about pop music to be able to talk to them about that, and she found them to be a pair of thoroughly professional actors.

Observer critic Philip Frank found the other parts caricatures 'in the coarse Joan Littlewood Brechtian manner'.[50] That could only be true of the men, and even then there is a joviality about it. Stephen Lewis (the immortal 'Blakey' of *On the Buses*) is the special constable who comes to get Charlie Kray (senior) to go and fight Hitler. Susan recalled that 'Tom Bell had to have his head blown off one day. He was sitting around between shots, with all this extraordinary muck, big gory bits hanging out of his head and he had forgotten about it completely. He was eating a red pudding. It was like he was eating his head. It was bizarre.' [51]

The women, a 'quartet of East End harpies' [52] are very convincing. Billie Whitelaw leads as Violet, the mother, and Susan plays her sister Rose. Alfred Lynch, playing Violet's husband, says of Susan: 'I loved acting but rarely enjoyed it, whereas she so obviously loved *and* enjoyed it.' [53] Aunt Rose was 'the wild one with the gypsy looks',[54] famous for having had an hour-long fistfight with two women (she won). Susan did some fighting that was cut out of the final version. 'I finished filming my part in *The Krays* down the road recently,' she said, speaking from her flat in Hackney, 'which involved a fierce fight. They didn't teach us how to land on pavements in the RSC.' [55] We see her throw a young doctor aside, in the hospital from which Violet is removing young Ronnie. Having nothing but each other, as Violet says, they defend each other fiercely. Rose, although very poor, is always giving the kids presents, including toy crocodiles.

---

[50] Philip Frank, *Observer*, 29.4.90
[51] Diana Robinson, *The Times* 26.4.90
[52] Ibid.
[53] Alfred Lynch, letter to author, 16.12.99
[54] John Pearson, *The Profession of Violence*, Panther 1973, p.26
[55] Hugh Montgomery-Massingberd, 'Meeting Mollycoddle', *Weekend Telegraph*, 11.11.89

This introduces the theme of domesticated monsters. Reg gives his fiancee Frances a silver crocodile brooch. She likes it, but on looking into Reg's eyes, says she sees monsters there. As one outside the quartet of Vi, her sisters and Grandma Lee, Frances is the only one to see what the Krays get up to, as the film has it, and it drives her to suicide. Rose, like Violet, sees no evil and makes no enquiry into the men's world of work. She knew the twins for twenty-four years.

As a working-class woman, she ages fast. The make-up, by Jennifer Boost, fills this in wonderfully well. My childhood was spent in Shepherds Bush, West London, in the fifties and that is a condition close enough to the East End to tell me that Sue got the cockney accent just right and all the mannerisms of a working-class woman: the artlessness of the hands left dangling; the self-mockery when they get up in their finery for a night at the club and the sense of enjoyable theatre that comes over them all down there (Jimmy Jewell, as grandpa Cannonball Lee, singing 'Balling the Jack'). After the wedding of Frances and Reg, Susan has one big speech. Sitting in Violet's dining-room, all dolled up, her face starts working. 'What's the matter, Rose?'

> *'I was just thinking. You know, I was on the bus the other day, and some ol' toe-rag was boasting about all he'd suffered in the war – stupid ol'-! – I'll tell you they don't know. It was the women that had the war, the real war. The women were left at home in the shit, not sittin' in some sparkling plane or gleaming tank. There was no glamour for them. They should have been with me when old Pauline Woolley went into labour. D' you remember that, Vi? Seven hours screaming down Bethnal Green bloody tube station. Then I had to cut the baby's head off to save the mother's life. She died anyway, poor old cow. God, there was so much blood. Jesus! And the abortions. Those poor girls. One day they'll drain Victoria Park lake, and you know what they'll find? What glorious remnants of the Second World War? Babies, that's what. Bullets and dead babies. Men! Mum's right. They stay kids all their fucking lives and they end up heroes, or monsters. Either way they win. Women have to grow up. If they stay children, they become victims.'*

This is an awful speech, beyond its physical horror. Husband Charlie, who has been bundled out of the room for being drunk, is neither a hero nor a monster. A monster has just married Frances and will keep her as a child and make her into the victim that Rose describes, but the women prefer not to know it. Their division of men into wimps and bastards is partly responsible. The speech is delivered with tremendous power, partly in a high, cracked voice, tremulous with tears, and partly in a savage snarl.

She got 'fucking' dead right. Us Cockneys, who use the word quite a lot, can never accept anyone else's pronunciation of it, either in the pallid, neutral way of educated people or a yokel's 'fook'. For the connoisseur, Steve Berkoff got it right performing in his own play *East*, talking about the "fuckin' 'orrible" sweaters sold in his shop. After her speech, Rose has a coughing fit, and the next we see of her she is expiring on her deathbed (of leukaemia). She 'fought death as she had fought everyone'.[56]

Susan was at least the equal of Billie Whitelaw in her portrayal of a tough woman, and that is high praise. It was presumably her gritty quality that made Doris Lessing choose her to make a recording of her short novel *Fifth Child* (1988, recording 1989). Susan found it technically difficult. Taking it on as a challenge, she found it cost her 'three months of sweat.'[57] She doesn't mention the content. It is a bloodcurdling tale of a fifth child arriving in an apparently happy, well-adjusted family of four children. The new boy is simply a monster, born without a set of normal reactions. He looks curiously at the others watching television, quite unable to see what it is they are responding to. He imitates their singing by roaring. They laugh at him, and that makes him uglier than ever. He terrorises the family pets, then the children, then the parents. He is quite ready to kill. He is like a throwback from some earlier stage of the human race, posing a perfectly insoluble problem, as Regan does to King Lear – 'Is there any cause in nature that makes these hard hearts?'

---

[56] Jon Pearson, op. cit. p. 109
[57] James Parker, *Sunday Times* 12.4.87

There was a radio excursion into horror with Don Taylor's radio play, *Exorcism* (December 1992). Susan plays a normal middle-class housewife who becomes a medium, in touch with the supernatural. It is a well-calculated Christmas ghost story with a moral, and chilly as only radio drama can be, the powers of suggestion not relying on the appearance of some unconvincing digital monster. Radio plays can be put together quite quickly, but Don Taylor recalls Susan as a 'thought-provoking actress, asking relevant questions and coming up with satisfying answers'.[58]

Susan is Rachel, hostess to a Christmas gathering of four, in a cottage in the country. She plays the harpsichord, when eerie and melancholy music comes to her, out of nowhere. They are comfortably off people, enjoying the usual Christmas fare, when the wine suddenly turns into blood, and the turkey becomes abominably hot. The harpsichord music returns, with nobody at the keyboard. Rachel sees the skeleton of a child on the bed upstairs. There is a power cut, and some force keeps them all there. Rachel is the only one to attempt to understand what is going on. She is possessed by the spirit of Sarah Jane Mulby, who starved to death in that cottage back in the eighteenth century. She cannot write, so she resolves to speak 'if only to the bare walls'. Her husband was hanged for burning the squire's barn. Rachel's voice pours out her grief and rage in a long, riveting speech. Sarah Jane looked in at the squire's window, where the family was feasting and the daughter playing the harpsichord:

> '*while on the same planet, in the same village, people are starving ... where there was no conscience, there was no hope ... I used to believe in God ... I have no forgiveness for the selfishness and greed which has destroyed my family ... someone, surely, must pay for our unjust deaths ... let my words burn themselves into the fabric of these walls, this cry of injustice from the dark centuries ... let someone, somewhere, remember.*'

Next we hear a news item. The Third World is getting poorer. Four people have been found starved to death in a well-stocked country cottage.

---

[58] Don Taylor, letter to author 13.12.99

The last of Susan's great ladies was Lady Russell, in the television film of *Persuasion* (1995). This began the great Jane Austen revival. It may still rank as the best adaptation of her novels. Roger Michell, director of *The Buddha of Suburbia*, had admired this particular novel for its melancholy and autumnal charm. He enlisted Nick Dear as a writer, although he hadn't done a love story before. No trouble or expense was spared. The costumes by Alexandra Byrne were all hand-made, down to the last detail; no Velcro. They won many awards, as did the whole production (including a Bafta). Only one man in the country could raise and lower a genuine chandelier with a full load of candles; he was hired.

Corin Redgrave recalls:

> '*Persuasion was filmed in September and October 1994, when the woods in Oxfordshire and Gloucestershire were beginning to turn yellow. Farringdon Hall, the stately home of Lord and Lady Farringdon was the location for Kellynch, Sir Thomas Eliot's country seat. In Jane Austen's story Sir Thomas is up to his ears in debt and tried to make economies. This being half way through Sir John Birt's reign at the BBC, harsh economies were being implemented there too, which meant no caravans or trailers were provided for the actors, nor any separate changing facilities. We all had to undress in the wardrobe van, and were lent a very cheerless room in the servants quarters to act as a green room. That was where I first met Susan Fleetwood.*' [59]

Maggie Smith had been offered the part of Lady Russell. She might have had a twinge of regret, seeing how well the whole production turned out. With hindsight, perhaps, Susan's face looks drawn, but she is as tall and imposing as ever. Lady Russell is a slow and deliberate creature of the old school, and dressed more in eighteenth-century fashion than Regency, with a complex collection of sombre fabrics, and some awesome hats. She shares the seriousness of Anne (Amanda Root) and one feels her deploring Sir Walter's betrayal of the standards of refinement he is supposed to maintain.

---

[59] Corin Redgrave, letter to author 18.12.00

Corin Redgrave showed his underestimated talent for comedy by playing Sir Walter with more than a touch of Toad. Towering a head over Anne, Lady Russell solemnly recommends the false Mr Elliott, but at a card party at the end she tells Anne to stick by a decision, and gain happiness.

'Lady Russell, Ann Elliot's mentor and friend,' writes Corin Redgrave, 'is a very difficult part, a near-irreconcilable contradiction. On the one hand Austen describes her as kindly and comfortably warmhearted, providing that mixture of affection and good sense which Anne, who is motherless, needs and which are notably lacking in her father's repertoire of emotion. On the other hand, like Sir Thomas, Lady Russell is an old-fashioned sort. In this capacity she inflicts much more damage on Anne than her father could ever manage. Anne could have survived her father's disdain for Captain Wentworth's humble origins. She might simply have eloped with him. Whereas Lady Russell was her trusted friend, so her disapproval effectively killed Anne's hopes of marrying Wentworth.

It is a clever irony and a true one, that each man – and in Jane Austen each woman – kills the thing he loves. But very hard to play. Especially if one is as delicate and tender as Susan Fleetwood. But she rescued what might have seemed a mismatched piece of acting by adding a dimension which is certainly not present in Jane Austen or even hinted at. She made Lady Russell mysterious, secretive, hard to fathom. She suggested that her conscience was very uneasy. She had caused her young friend terrible unhappiness and was trying to make amends.' [60]

There was much happiness in the production. Susan took to Fiona Finlay, the producer, instantly. On hearing that Fiona had just won an award for a documentary (*Black Day for the Bride*, on Alzheimer's disease), Sue ordered up champagne for an instant party. There were several old hands from the RSC on the set, John Woodvine (as Admiral Croft), Amanda Root and Simon Russell Beale, so she felt quite at home. Corin Redgrave did and didn't consider himself an RSC actor. He didn't know Susan's work, as 'for fifteen years I hardly went to

---

[60] Corin Redgrave, ibid.

the theatre, and never to the RSC. Theatre made me nostalgic for acting, from which I had been banished, more or less, for my political activity'.[61]

Susan's socialising had to be limited even more than before, as the need to conserve energy was greater. As with Stratford at the time of *Much Ado*, her ever-helpful mother took a cottage, this time near Bath, so that Susan could rest up. Like most of them, Corin Redgrave didn't know she was ill. He recalls her eating 'a vile concoction of alfalfa and beans out of a tupperware box. When I thoughtlessly, tactlessly, teased her about this dreadful diet, she made a funny face and said yes, it was just as boring as it looked, but it was "good for her insides." How could I not have known that she was ill? Because, I suppose, Susan gave one permission not to know, not to trouble oneself about it, to believe that whatever the problem was, or had been, it was being dealt with, it was well under control.'[62]

Once Susan had relinquished Shakespeare, she was hardly ever to play the romantic lead; even *Chandler and Co* follows the pattern of putting her to one side in those stakes. As she herself noted, there is a dearth of modern writing good enough to offer those parts:

> '*I need my daily shot of something real, emotional and committed. Modern writing doesn't do that. I can only tune in when love, hate, anger and sadness are close. Even when I'm not working I read them and act them…*'[63]

The Forsyte Saga is unfortunately representative of modern writing in the manner of stifling emotion. Priestley's *Dangerous Corner*, and even so modern a piece as Mortimer's *Summer's Lease* follow it in treating strong emotion as a dark, unimaginable thing. The plot is spent in investigating how it was possible at all. It isn't rendered directly, and that is exactly where Susan would have scored.

The best modern vehicle she actually found was Michael Frayn's *Landing on the Sun*, a novel adapted by him for the small screen, shown in June 1994. It is still,

[61] Corin Redgrave, ibid.
[62] Corin Redgrave, ibid.
[63] Dominc Gray 'A Fleeting Glimpse', *What's On*, October 1988

precisely, a post-mortem of a strange love affair. It begins as a civil service security enquiry, but the investigator Brian Jessel (Robert Glenister, looking the very incarnation of shrewdness) becomes obsessively interested in what actually happened between his predecessor in the Cabinet Office, Steven Summerchild (Roger Allam), and Elizabeth Serafin (Sue), an Oxford philosophy don. (There is a credibility problem here. I do not believe that from the founding of Oxford in the twelfth century there has ever been a don to bear a semblance, be it ever so faint, of Susan's beauty. I have the same trouble regarding nuns and Audrey Hepburn.)

On Harold Wilson's return to office in 1974, these respectable individuals had been suddenly deputed to set up a unit to investigate 'the quality of life'. Elizabeth is rung up at home and told 'It's the prime minister!' 'The prime minister? In what sense?' No details were forthcoming. They are assigned a couple of poky rooms in the labyrinths of Whitehall, where they sit and discuss the concept of happiness. She gets excited by the notion, going down the palatial main stairs dropping oranges from her shopping bag, exclaiming 'It may prove just as hard to look at directly as the sun is … all our ideas revolve around it … the idea of happiness is like the sun at the centre of the planetary system. It is the notion that holds the whole system together. The Americans have put a man on the moon. We must launch our rocket and go one better. We must make an expedition to the sun!'

They try to verify happiness from their own experience. She talks hypothetically of their being lovers, in a restaurant, gazing at each other over a bottle of wine. There is such warmth and charm in the way she projects hypotheses that the outcome is inevitable. A dying anchorite would have to respond. Elizabeth's husband, another professional philosopher, never speaks to her about anything, and she never knows where her three children are. We next see Summerchild playing the violin to her – not very well – and her weeping on the sofa, saying 'What are we going to do?' They make the rooms into a little home, and get out onto the roof to sunbathe and have lunch. As he organises that, she affectionately tells him to go away and let her work; she goes into a whispered soliloquy for a tape recorder (the tapes forming the basis for Jessel's investigation). It is lightly and gently ecstatic, as she gets to the concept through emotion:

> 'I want to say this now, while it's still fresh in my mind. When I turned around and I knew it would be him, and it was him, that was happiness. When he put his head through that hatch, knowing that I would be here, and I was here, and he smiled, that was happiness. It is happiness still, now, as I say these words. I am at this moment happy, whatever may happen in the future, however my understanding of the world changes. I know it with the absolute certainty that philosophers have always longed to find.'

Frances Tite, Summerchild's boss (Patrick Godfrey) susses out that something has gone wrong; he attacks indirectly, in the English manner, by changing the locks and withdrawing their security passes. Summerchild, who used to be a climber, breaks into the office on a weekend. On Monday morning he is on the roof, saluting the dawn and looking for a way down. He falls, and is fatally injured. Elizabeth's doings after this remain shrouded in mystery. It is a very light sketch of a love affair, in the chilly environs of Whitehall, but it is moving in the way that Chekhov's short stories can be moving. Susan's performance chimes with what she said about Kate in *Taming of the Shrew*, having 'rather a holy, rather a simple, rather solemn, lovely experience … ' At the end of her career, looking as gorgeous as ever, but with very little time to live, she can sound the note of pure idealism about romantic love.

One project she had in mind for the future deserves mention, since it so closely paralleled her own situation. It was to be a staged version of the correspondence between George Sand and Flaubert, adapted by Peter Eyre from a translation by Frances Steegmuller and Barbara Bray of 1993. This was produced as *Cher Maitre* at the Almeida Theatre in the summer of 1999, with Peter Eyre as Flaubert and Irene Worth as George Sand. The programme pays tribute to 'the inspiration of Susan Fleetwood', who would of course have played George Sand. George Sand was 53 when she met Flaubert, seventeen years his senior, 'too old for their affection to degenerate into a love affair'.[64] They seldom met over the

---

[64] Peter Eyre, programme notes to *Cher Maitre* July 1999

next nineteen years, but the correspondence meant a good deal to both of them. She always said there was a feminine side to him, a great tenderness amidst his artistic anguish and black rages against politics and journalists. He saw a masculine strength in her compassion. She was as romantic as she had ever been, and carried a serenity that studiously ignored encroaching illness. She said she liked actors:

> '*I feel for them what I feel for the woods and the fields, for everything and everybody … It's amidst all these that I make my life, and as I love my life I love everything that sustains and stimulates this. I realise people are nasty to me sometimes, but I don't feel it any more. I know bushes have thorns, but that doesn't ever stop me thrusting my hands in them and finding flowers.*' [65]

She never told Flaubert quite how ill she was, and when she died in June 1876 he hadn't finished the story he had hoped would please her, 'Un Coeur Simple'.

Peter Eyre knew how little time Susan had. He asked her over dinner if she was ill and she burst into tears. He was one of very few that she confided in. 'You have friends,' she said, 'you go out; I don't.' The others who knew, apart from family, tended to be those who knew the awfulness of fatal illness themselves or in their loved ones. One was Francis Barber, who was with Susan on the recording of *Daughters of Venice* in 1994. Francis had recently lost her mother and brother, the latter in an accident. In the Green Room at the BBC they talked and Sue suddenly confided that she had not long to live. (Francis hopes very much that this doesn't hurt friends who knew Susan better than she, but didn't hear.) They bewailed the uselessness of men, the shortage of good roles, the shortness of life, and the state of the ashtrays. They talked themselves into such a state of despair that they burst out laughing and resolved to totter off to see a play together some time like 'two old spinsters'. They managed it once, at the Hampstead Everyman. Sue recommended Tibetan Buddhism, bells and chanting and all, but it was not Francis' cup of tea. Sue was also listening to self-cure tapes, where syrupy

---

[65] *The Letters of Gustave Flaubert and George Sand*, ed. Alphone Jacob, transl. F. Steegmuller, B. Bray, Harvill Press 1999, p.121

American voices tell you you can be filled with good health by thinking good thoughts; death is a consumer's option.

Still, one fervently hopes that there were scraps of comfort from all this. Sally Dexter (fellow-actor on *A Few Short Journeys of the Heart*) was interested in Buddhism; Sue and she talked about it. Sue had gone into it quite seriously, as she went into everything. She made *The Tibetan Book of Living and Dying* one of the very few books she ever bothered with. It offers a philosophic way of meeting death calmly; reincarnation plays a part. It suited her because it didn't have an elaborate metaphysic, and was more a science of the mind than a world-view.

In May 1993 she went with Richard Cottrell to hear the Dalai Lama lecture at Wembley. She heard him say that 'You must identify the disturbing emotion as your real enemy … Anger is the most serious problem facing the world today'. She must have felt a lot of anger at the illness that had taken her so young. Before arriving at resignation, she had of course fought the disease with all her great strength. There is an ice-pack treatment applied to the head, to prevent the hair-loss that follows the use of the drug Doxorubicin; as it reaches -20 degrees, most people can only stand it once. Susan took it eight times; it took days to recover from it. Driving back from chemotherapy with her old friend Rosemary Marter, she laughed at the way her hair was still coming out. Only those who have cancer can know what that means.

Susan had a lot of experience of helping other sufferers, such as her great friend, the actress Brenda Bruce, who lost two husbands and a son to disease. Sue had also been a great comfort to Janet Grainger, Gawn Grainger's wife. 'The dying comfort the dying, as it were'. The first Christmas after Janet had been diagnosed, Susan phoned to make sure their son Charlie would be in to receive a present. It was a pair of drumsticks – Charlie being a drummer in a small band – delivered by Mick Fleetwood, perhaps the most famous rock drummer in the world. It was three years before that when Sue had confided in Gawn.

> *'The doorbell went. I was in the bath. I towel wrapped and answered the door. There was Susan.*
> *"G…" (she didn't use my full name she always called me 'G') Can I come*

in?"

"I'm in the bath."

"That's alright."

We went back to the bathroom. She sat on the edge of the bath and I got back in. Brother and sister. There was a pause, a single tear rolled down her cheek. I stared up at her. Then very quietly but firmly, she said, "I'm going to die, G." I continued to stare. "Cancer... don't tell anyone. I need to work." Two weeks before she died she came for tea. She was tired, very tired. "I don't think I'm going to make it G," she said. I never saw her again.' [66]

She made a round of visits to see old friends like Gawn. She rang up Lila Kaye, from her early days at the RSC, asking to speak to 'Old Smelly Boots', so that Lila knew at once who it was. She went to see Frances de la Tour and Maggie Smith when they were in *Three Tall Women*. She went to a reunion of Acter people at the Kenilworth Hotel in Great Russell Street in January 1995. She was photographed there, looking as good as ever. Tim Piggott-Smith and Juliet Ayckroyd thought she looked well, although Juliet saw her dipping into a large handbag for pills. 'It felt as though she wanted to reach out and make contact with us.' [67] 'Now that I realise she was dying', writes Corin Redgrave, and '[she] knew that she was dying, and simply wanted to live as long and as beautifully as she could, I am filled with admiration. At the great risk of sounding affected, mystical and pseudo-fanatic, I must say that I know now that Susan's life must have been fine, because no one could die so finely who had not lived finely.' [68]

When she could no longer look after herself at her Hackney flat, even with visits from her mother, she went back to the family home in Salisbury.

She always got on well with her cockney builder, Ron Davies (called 'Mr Snoz' because of his sinus trouble; he called her 'Miss Silicone Chip' because she was a dab hand with the stereo). She gave him a big farewell hug. 'I'm going away to

[66] Gawn Grainger, letter to author 1998
[67] Interview Juliet Ayckroyd 6.6.97
[68] Corin Redgrave, op. cit.

get better'. He knew what she meant. 'I am so proud to have know this lady, my friend,' he says.[69]

She told Michael Gough that she would be 'like a little bird, just flying away'.

Susan died in Salisbury on September 29th 1995. In death she looked 'like an empress', according to Rosemary Marter.

The wild English Rose who was somehow also Caliban; the chaste Marina who was also the Viennese wife who went into graphic orgasms; the rowdy Lady Rodolpha with her woolie-wambles who was also a crazed and grubby Ophelia; the Aunt Rose who would trade curses and punches with anyone, who was also the dowager Lady Russell; all these roles fade away with her, like the spirits on a Tintoretto canvas, who vanish into wreathes of smoke, turning into sketches in the air around the living people.

'She was always young,' writes Gawn Grainger, 'and now always will be'.

The news burst upon an ignorant and startled theatre world. Charles Dance, reading his paper in a transatlantic plane, was shocked to see her obituary. John Theocaris, who had been at RADA with Sue, was looking over papers in the BBC office in Washington DC 'when suddenly my heart stopped. There was Sue, looking lovely and radiant, in the center of her obituary notice.'[70] Paul Webster, driving to work at the Chichester Festival Theatre, heard the news on his radio and 'gasped in disbelief'.

'It is commonly observed,' writes Dr. Johnson, 'that among soldiers and seamen, though there is much kindness, there is little grief; they see their friends fall without any of that lamentation which is indulged in security and idleness, because they have no leisure to spare from the care of themselves.'[71] Among actors, too, there is much kindness, and although acting is not quite the same

---

[69] Ron Davies, letter to author 6.2.00
[70] John Theocaris, letter to author 21.5.99
[71] Dr. Samuel Johnson, Rambler No. 47, Yale Edition of the *Works of Samuel Johnson*, ed. W.J. Bate and Albrecht B. Strauss, Yale University Press, 1969, Vol.III p.257.

emergency as battle, Sue would have agreed that the show must go on, and her friends were very busy.

Ian Richardson recalls that he 'heard of her death just as I was about to make my entrance in "The Miser" at the Theatre Royal, Bath, and I can tell you that playing a farce after a body blow like that was not easy. The house was good and at the end I made a little speech, dedicating the applause to her'.[72]

Richard Moore heard 'just before a matinee at Chichester of *The Visit* directed, oddly enough, by Terry Hands. It was a grim afternoon for those of us who'd known her and I remember standing upstage in the dark next to an actor who was sobbing and saying, "I can't believe it.".'[73]

Catherine Russell had had some forewarning. She was appearing as Masha in *The Three Sisters*, at the Bristol Old Vic. She went on to the stage, gazed into an empty auditorium and dedicated her next performance to her:

"This one's for you, Sue."[74]

[72] Ian Richardson, letter to author 21.5.99
[73] Richard Moore, letter to author 8.9.97
[74] Catherine Russell, phone interview 21.12.99

VIII. "An Ocean Liner of a Lady"

ANY YOUNG ACTRESS STEPPING OUT OF DRAMA SCHOOL who had been promised a career like this would be delighted: a good training in rep; years with the great national companies; constant film and television work, including some with a director of European reputation; forays into the West End. And yet...

And yet there is cause for regret. With all this work and constant fine reviews, why was she not famous? John Fernald was disappointed in her career. It is not just that she died too young, although it is a practical certainty that had she lived she could have gone on to play the remaining great classical roles: Medea, Clytemnestra, Volumnia. She might have been made a Dame. Judi Dench only attained her international reputation in her sixties, although as soon as she took to the British stage her star quality had been obvious. Terry Hands thinks that Susan should have stayed at the RSC throughout, rising to a height as Queen Margaret in the *Henry VI* plays which he put on in 1977, emulating Peggy Ashcroft's triumph in that role in 1963/4. This is a very austere vision. These plays are not great showcases, containing much early and inferior verse. John Barton had had to revise them extensively to make Peggy's triumph possible.

I like to think of Susan most as Cleopatra. She could have been the 'lass unparalleled' that her servant Charmian speaks of. It would have been but a few steps on from the Beatrice she consolidated in 1990. It is of course a hugely difficult play to mount. Margaret Leighton was Cleo in 1969, Janet Suzman in 1972, Glenda Jackson in 1978/9, Helen Mirren in 1982 and Judi Dench in 1987. Asked in 1990 if she had any Shakespearean schemes, Susan replied 'Only a very private one ... I would be very disappointed on my deathbed if I hadn't played a Cleopatra'.[1] It was said with a laugh, to close an interview, but it was another instance of her joking about something very serious. She told Peter Eyre that she

---

[1] Sheridan Morley, Arts Programme, BBC Radio 2, 2.9.90

thought the RSC owed it to her to give her the part. She had the looks, of course, including the stature that would have been a great asset. She had sensuality in abundance and she had the formidable quality that an empress would need. She told her friend Rosemary that her men had all chosen her; she hadn't chosen any of them, but they all turned out in the end to be frightened of her. One doesn't imagine Terry Hands, especially, scaring easy, so this must be fear in a special sense.

My fictional parallel to the young Susan, Henry James's Nanda, scared the wits out of Vanderbank, a young man with every conceivable worldly advantage. 'I'm just too powerful for them', Susan would say calmly, of certain companies and directors; she was not one for false modesty. Her brother Mick said of her:

> *'I see something of myself in Susan ... In the way people are frightened of us.*
> *I think it's to do with childhood, the way we didn't have to fight our parents...*
> *She works. She won't compromise. And yet she's not as severe as people think.*
> *She's powerful, and that's the danger. People are wary of powerful,*
> *professional women. But I'm her brother and I know she's a paradox. I'm*
> *aware of a very, very pithy underbelly there. I know she's soft. She expects a*
> *lot. A lot of a man. She can eat a man up and spit him out. I wouldn't*
> *imagine it's an easy job, being her boyfriend. She throws herself into her work*
> *with dogged resolve to do it, accomplish it, and that's it. I imagine her dream*
> *would be to be as gloriously committed to a relationship. Susan is the one*
> *who says "I want to talk to you" ... She won't take it that I'm just fine. She*
> *wants the absolute truth...'* [2]

He once took her to a pop star wedding in California where George Harrison was one of the guests. Susan came away with vituperation for him. 'He wasn't making any sense!' We recall her knocking the actress about on the set of *Much Ado*. She was invariably kind and affectionate with her nieces and nephews, and Sebastian's son Luke, but she was intolerant of lapses of manners, mumbling, for instance. 'Are you talking to me?' she would ask, icily.

---

[2] Sally Vincent, 'Relative Values', *Sunday Times*, 29.1.84

Another quality she would have had to have for Cleopatra, and did have, is a kind of licensed theatricality. There is no point in asking if Shakespeare's Cleopatra is genuine or fake. She is an actress every minute of the day, in the public eye from when she appears on the barge to when she commits suicide, two pieces of equal showmanship. Susan had her critics, who thought that she was an average company person, with the usual actressy mannerisms. Someone as fond of her as Mike Newell said he never knew when Susan was real or fake. She would talk of the dangers in acting, and he would ask her if she meant the sort of danger faced by soldiers or miners; how could acting be equally real?[3] She once said of herself:

> *'I like being able to fool around in the wings and be sassy, telling jokes and flirting about, and then go on stage and be completely involved in another aspect of life altogether, crying and genuinely feeling absolutely destroyed, and then coming off, still completely soaked in tears, being able to say something flippant. But these moods are genuine at the time. There's always one part of us that's aloof, watching, both when we're acting and in real life.'[4]*

'Tis sweating labour/ To bear such idleness so near the heart.'

One actor thought that in another profession, she'd have been called a manic depressive. Having caught such self-dramatisation in Anna Arkadina, and made it objective, Susan could surely have turned it into an instrument to beguile her Mark Antony.

'If you find him sad, / Say I am dancing; if in mirth, report/ That I am sudden sick...'

On hearing that Susan wanted to be Cleopatra, Sister Olive said 'She won't get it. She won't push herself for it'. She never was political. (Terry Hands denies that being so gets you anywhere in the theatre, but whenever I repeat this remark it elicits howls of derision). There was a time when Susan might have been Hedda Gabler, but she refused the part, like a horse refusing a fence; she just would not

---

[3] Phone interview Mike Newell 8.6.99
[4] Vera Lustig, 'Diva', *Plays and Players* Feb. 1991

do it. A more political actress would have taken it. When Sebastian used to urge her to go out to parties and make contacts, she said she preferred to stay by the fire with a cup of tea. Her agent Duncan Heath says she used to make fun of the idea of going to Hollywood to be 'part of the scene'. She caught a glimpse of what a film-star's life would be like when she appeared in *The Sacrifice*, and disliked it. She also had Mick's career before her, to see what superstardom could mean.

If she had played a great Cleopatra, how much difference would it have made? It wasn't all that much help for Judi Dench when she succeeded in the role, against expectation. The days are gone when Shakespeare on the stage was the road to stardom. McKellan may turn out to be the last actor to have taken it. No Shakespearean production can hope to make headline news in the way that Peter Brook's *Midsummer Night's Dream* did in 1970. Society doesn't look to see itself reflected in so complex and subtle an image as Cleopatra. Olivier now looks as though he had more than a touch of Vincent Crummles about him, and perhaps, as with Vincent, the idea of the British Empire behind him was essential to his profile. That has gone, to be replaced by various versions of multiculturalism.

Terry Hands, Mike Newell and Blodwen Doyle (the cleaner at the Everyman) all think of Susan first and last as a Shakespearian actress. Sebastian Graham-Jones and Bill Bryden, who knew Susan very well, and worked with her at the National, dispute this. If she had had the chance to do more comedy, she might have ended with a quite different image. Frances de la Tour has played Cleopatra recently, but it did not wipe out the memory of her as Miss Jones in *Rising Damp*; nor should it.

Actors of an older generation, Olivier, Richardson and Peggy Ashcroft, had started film careers early, to run in tandem with stage work, a wise career move. One reason why Susan did not do this was that in the sixties, with a film like *Darling* counting as a major work, films were, as Duncan Heath says, 'on the floor'. By 1974, at the latest, Susan was aware of the need to do more films and television. Her main film had a director who will always be a cult figure, but never widely popular. Her fine achievements in *Summer's Lease* and *Landing on the Sun* didn't catch on, and very little tv drama gets recycled. Director Desmond

Davis thinks that TV requires fixed personalities who never change or develop. (One thinks, cheerily, of *Dad's Army*.) Film needs similar people, with the added longing to be a superstar. Susan's very versatility counted against her. She was a great stage actress, born out of her time and place, perhaps; Moscow or Paris in the 1890's might have been ideal for her. She didn't have the easy pathos of an Audrey Hepburn, who could look like a little waif and stray even when dressed like a million dollars. (That works two ways, of course – who could resist a pretty waif who might turn out to be a princess?) Hepburn was pretty much the same from one film to another, which was fine, because that personality was so completely delightful that one could never get enough of it anyway. Would that she had had time for a dozen more films! Susan's size, for one thing, meant that obvious bids for pathos were ruled out.

On the other hand, she lacked aggression. Michael Billington thinks that some actresses have an oddly distinctive quality that makes them determined to subdue audiences into liking them. Peggy Ashcroft used to shake her fist at the auditorium before the crowd came. (Susan would acclimatise herself to them gradually, listening to them assemble over the tannoy.) Another famous actress used to calm herself by sewing obsessively on a cushion. Asked what she was sewing, she showed the lettering – 'fuck 'em all'.

Ben Kingsley thinks that what Susan had, beyond her beauty, was a kind of eccentricity. Ronald Pickup says that 'inside every great beauty there is an old bag trying to get out'. Perhaps Susan's did with Aunt Rose in *The Krays*. Another asset Susan did not have was the simple incisive image of the modern feminist, in a world where women especially are told 'ya gotta be cool, ya gotta be tough, ya gotta be strong', etc. Helen Mirren has just enough of that, an air of self-possession, a charm and a sensuality that loses nothing in Fortune's and men's eyes by being finely calculated. '*Her* a sex goddess!' was Susan's comment.

Bill Bryden thinks that Susan knew herself to be in the top elite of acting, a body never to be found all in one place or play, but existent, a kind of actors' Valhalla. On the everyday level, however, doing without fame was not easy, and Susan did her share of grumbling. 'All those years of slugging my guts out for the RSC, and where did it get me?' There was never much money. She hoped for an award for her Beatrice or her Anna Arkadina, but no. As sister Sally was showing her around an exhibition once, Susan inveighed against the miseries of being an actress and said a painter must find life easier. Apparently they have traumas of their own.

In 1980 Robert Cushman paid Susan the very singular tribute that she was 'the most enchanting actress never to crack a smile'.[5] On a literal level, it is quite easy to refute this. He was thinking of the roles she had played at the National between 1975 and 1979, where the figure of the woman as victim recurs and recurs. This is a fault in modern writing. 'They know not how to touch the heart save by wounding it.' The production photos alone, from other plays, *Love's Labour's Lost*, *Taming of the Shrew*, *As You Like It*, and *The Recruiting Officer* show glorious laughter. She had triumphed with her Portia and Rosalind. When playing a very tragic Ophelia in 1972, she was also playing the earthy and cheerful Lady Rodolpha. In 1982, along with her Titania, there was the comically vulgar June in *Way Upstream*. Her culminating stage roles were Beatrice and the satirically observed Anna Arkadina.

Much of this was rooted in her enormous enjoyment of life. In the file of letters I have from actors, there are many who say, 'I didn't know Susan at all well, but what I do remember about her is her warmth and laughter'. Her favourite comedian was Tommy Cooper, for his real skill as well as his patter.

She genuinely enjoyed company life enormously, the quick, close bonds that can be formed, the vagaries and mistakes of the rehearsal process. She was the ideal company member, the absolute antithesis of the prima donna. She got angry with herself far more than with other people, when things weren't going right. No tantrums, never late and first off the book, despite dyslexia. Stage fright never left her, but she didn't bother her directors with it.

From Acter days, Martin Best recalls her being called 'Fleeters', a 'thoroughly good chap'. In New York, the whole company went out to see a skin flick, which

---

[5] Robert Cushman, *Observer*, 13.4.80

much amused them. Michael Bogdanov says he and Sue could hardly be in conversation a few minutes before they were laughing and joking at the absurdities of life and people. Catherine Russell recalls a wicked sense of humour. When an actor made a very theatrical entrance on *Chandler and Co* she turned to Catherine and said 'pass the chocs and the programme, darling,' in a Sybil Fawlty voice. She enjoyed banter with close friends like Brenda Bruce, whom she called 'the old boot' – 'I'm just off to see the old boot'. Her flat in Hackney was called 'Fleetwood Towers', and although people didn't call in casually, there were parties, with music, where she kept guests well supplied with wine even after she had given it up.

Before she became ill she was a hearty eater and drinker. After a performance, a litre bottle of red wine could just disappear. Bill Bryden recalls her as drinking 'like a sailor'. If the bar was crowded and someone wanted to know what she wanted, she would shake her hand like a bell-ringer, for Bell's whisky. She and Sinead Cusack would down a couple of those in the Stratford 'Dirty Duck' now and again. As we know from Doyne Byrd and Brenda Blethyn, Susan had a wonderful streak of vulgarity. ('If you don't like vulgarity', said the distinguished critic Santayana, 'what can you relish?'). Juliet Ayckroyd remembers Susan keeping them amused in the dressing room with Tampax jokes.

Her full self wasn't always there in her enthusiasms. Sometimes she laughed too much to cover shyness and with a shade too much anxiety in controlling the situation. Once in the Green Room at Stratford she was enthusing over a Russian camera she had bought. Her excitement was too much and too sustained for people, who drifted away. 'I always do that to people,' she mused. Sometimes it was as though her self only got constituted around whatever absorbed her, instead of her lending energy out from the central core. There was a vehemence about her, as if the laughter were a gift she made to other people, and a distraction from some pain within. She rarely led the laughter or the conversation in a group, although she would throw back her great mane of hair and laugh heartily at something that caught her.

Cushman was not wrong-*headed*. Some of her greatest triumphs were portraits of pain: Adelaide in *The Sacrifice*, Nora in *The Plough and the Stars*, the National's Ophelia. There were some melancholy touches in her Portia and Rosalind. Nobody could touch the heart like Susan Fleetwood. What she showed, again and again, was vulnerability. Sensuality was there in abundance, but there was great purity in her romantic emotions. As Pegeen Mike, Portia, Rosalind and Beatrice there was a surprise in her emotions, as though she had just been visited by them, and they opened up a world of possibilities. Her deep idealism came out in her understanding of Kate and Petruchio, and in her portrayal of Elizabeth Serafin, the philosopher who had discovered what happiness was. It feels like a youthful quality that she kept intact, deep down, as the years went by and disappointments accrued. It comes across as directly as the raw, ugly pain, the zestful vulgarity, and the horror she had to transmit in *The Sacrifice* or *Exorcism*.

Another actress would have bevelled the edges to make them more acceptable. If she had been interested in politics, like Vanessa Redgrave, or had had children, that might have taken away some of the burning energy she put into her acting. This might have made life easier for her, but it would have been the audience's loss. One actor commented that she only carried herself at her full height on stage.

Jonathan Hyde and Randal Herley described Sue's un-English quality of intensity as something Celtic or Continental; blood on both sides of her family supports this theory. On the other hand, Susan again and again gave portraits of middle-class women who were neurotically self-pitying, authors of their own misfortunes – Valeria, Varya, Bertha, Laura and Anna Arkadina (all Continentals – although the list possibly includes Pamela Redman, of *Don't Be Silly*). And among her gallery of portraits of decent Englishwomen like Molly Pargeter, disciplined self-suppression came out as something very attractive. That had its roots in her life, too. Paul Scofield writes:

'As an actress she never seemed to do anything for effect, she understated herself, presenting only the character she was playing with a kind of sidelong dismissal of her own presence. She was sustained by her work, self

advertisement she treated with sturdy disregard, and her attitude to that work, and the tenderness and sensitivity of her acting was for me a source of vast admiration – and of love … I miss her very much.' [6]

Juliet Stevenson says that the very greatest Shakespearean roles are still reserved for men. Even today, it is hard to imagine a lady playing Lear or Macbeth, in a full reversal of the Elizabethan situation. If fantasy were to prevail, and an actress were to get her chance at any hero, the one I would pick for Susan is the dyed-in-the-wool patrician, Coriolanus. Her mother likes to think of her as St. Joan, but I like to imagine her going all the way as a formidable soldier. I am thinking of his rugged unsociability, except among his elite profession, his honesty, his indifference to cheap praise, hearing his 'nothings monstered'; despite all of which, he was very close to his mother. He had the quality the Romans called 'terribilitas'. He was formidable because he was completely serious, and judged himself as harshly as he judged others.

Thus, she was able to meet every demand that Terry Hands made of her, and never make a fight of it, because she had strength in another sphere. Terry, like Peter Brook, had the Continental intellectual's mix of driving willpower wedded to highly articulate theory. Director's theatre, which Fernald had celebrated in the early sixties as a new opportunity, stands indicted by Simon Callow, in the nineties, as a tyranny, with a newer tyranny, that of the designer, threatening to take over. It took an actress as combative as Glenda Jackson to give as good as she got from Peter Brook. Susan had no theories and wasn't combative.

Nicholas Renton describes some actors as natural Buddhists, feeling their way intuitively towards the revelation of how to do their part by moving pencils, touching chairs, sniffing round a room as cats do, to take possession of it, very quietly evolving a world of emotion and imagination. Creatively, Susan transcended herself in this non-assertive fashion. Morally, she made the effort, through Tibetan Buddhism. At the end she was, she said, just like a little bird that would soon fly away. Mental concentration and great moral energy, perhaps a kind of sublimated anger, go into the suppression of the self. It's a quality that

---

[6] Paul Scofield, letter to author 5.12.99

cannot in the least advertise itself, which is precisely why it should be celebrated. The same discipline she cultivated as an actress helped her to fight her illness, extracting all she could from life up to the finish. She combined vast strength with great gentleness. This made her, as Terry Hands said, 'easy to love'. From the storm and stress of acting *The Plough and the Stars*, Carmel McSharry felt the same:

> 'I've only got one thing to say. When she was Nora, she had been very powerful, but she suddenly came across as being terribly vulnerable, as though her skin were made of tissue. At that moment I actually loved her. Moments like that – that's what you're in the game for.'[7]

If Susan was a spiritual aristocrat and a tragedienne, she was a figure for whom our Ab Fab culture has a limited tolerance. She was a dark jewel in the treasure-chest of British acting talent. Russell Davies called her 'a great ocean liner of a lady'. Several actors I spoke to called her a 'thoroughbred'. Let a great writer balance these metaphors. In Joseph Conrad's story *The Shadow Line*, a young captain gets his first glimpse of the ship he is to command:

> At first glance I saw that she was a high-class vessel, a harmonious creature in the lines of her fine body, in the proportioned tallness of her spars. Whatever her age and her history, she had preserved the stamp of her origin. She was one of those craft that, in virtue of their design and complete finish, will never look old. Amongst her companions moored to the bank, and all bigger than herself, she looked like a creature of high breed – an Arab steed in a string of carthorses. A voice behind me said in a nasty equivocal tone: "I hope you are satisfied with her, Captain." I did not even turn my head. It was the master of the steamer, and whatever he meant, whatever he thought of her, I knew that, like some rare women, she was one of those creatures whose mere existence is enough to awaken an unselfish delight. One feels that it is good to be in the world in which she has her being.

---

[7] Carmel McSharry, phone interview 30.4.98

It's implicit that nobody really owns such a creation, neither builders, nor agents, nor the captain. It stands as a testimony to something good in the human race.

I have looked at Venice from the bell tower of San Giorgio Maggiore and felt the same way. (Like all thoughts about Venice, this can't possibly be original.)

Of Susan Fleetwood, Conrad's last sentence rings true. Such rare women as she walk the earth. One may do so again, before too long.

The thought is enough to make one want to stick around.

Index

Photographs

Sue with Terry Hands and Stuart Richman in the cellar at the Everyman.

Criminals (1967) (photo: Reg Wilson; courtesy of the Shakespeare Birthplace Trust).

As Audrey in *As You Like It* (1968) Brian Robson as William, Patrick Stewart as Touchstone.

With Ian Richardson in *Pericles*, 1969 (courtesy of the Shakespeare Birthplace Trust).

As Marina in *Pericles*, 1969 (courtesy of the Shakespeare Birthplace Trust).

The Recruiting Officer, 1970, with Ian McKellan (courtesy of Chris Arthur).

Kate, *The Taming of the Shrew* 1973 (Reg Wilson; courtesy of the Shakespeare Birthplace Trust).

Portia, *The Merchant of Venice* 1972. (Reg Wilson; courtesy of the Shakespeare Birthplace Trust.)

Rosalind, *As You Like It* 1980. (Reg Wilson; courtesy of the Shakespeare Birthplace Trust.)

Rosalind, with John Bowe as Orlando, *As You Like It* 1980. (Reg Wilson; courtesy of the Shakespeare Birthplace Trust.)

Beth Crawford, the Burra Memsahib, *Heat and Dust* 1982 (courtesy of James Ivory).

Beatrice, *Much Ado about Nothing* 1990 (courtesy of Ivan Kyncl).

Ana Arkadina, *The Seagull* 1990 (courtesy of Ivan Kyncl).

Sue at her last Acter gathering 1995, with Bernard Lloyd (left) and Mr and Mrs Swander and below with David Rintoul and Homer Swander (photos courtesy of Laurie Asprey).

As Marina in *Pericles*, 1969 (courtesy of the Shakespeare Birthplace Trust).

A summary of Susan Fleetwood's theatre, radio, television and film roles

Specific roles in chronological order:

English Wild Rose Fairy, Joseph, Dixie (*Cat on a Hot Tin Roof*), Laurel (*Chalk Garden*), Hortensia (*Taming of the Shrew*), Caliban, Madam Y (*The Stronger*); **at Rada** Cleopatra, Lady Macbeth, Rosalind; **at the Everyman** Charlotta Ivanovna (*Cherry Orchard*), Lady Percy (*Henry IV Part One*), Chrous Leader (*Murder in the Cathedral*), Gwendolen (*Importance of Being Earnest*), Lady Macbeth (*Macbeth*), Polly Garter (*Under Milk Wood*), Beatrice (*Four Seasons*), Queen Margaret (*Richard III*), Emma Fezziwig (*Christmas Carol*), Margaret (*The Great God Brown*), Tino (*Hypochondriac*), Mrs Grigson (*Shadow of a Gunman*), Lis (*Fando and Lis*), Cyrenne (*Rattle of a Simple Man*), Estelle (*In Camera*), Alison (*Look Back in Anger*); **at the RSC** Natalya (*The Proposal*), Amanda (*The Relapse*), Beba (*Criminals*), Isbella (*Women Beware Women*), Regan (*King Lear*), Audrey (*As You Like It*), Margaret (*Much Ado*), Cassandra (*Troilus and Cressida*), Julia (*Two Gentlemen*), Thaisa/Marina (*Pericles*); **at Cambridge TC** Nina (*Seagull*), Sylvia (*Recruiting Officer*), Lady Rodolpha (*Man of the World*), Ophelia (*Hamlet*); **tv** Mary McDowell (*Watercress Girl*); **at Prospect TC** Ermentine (*You and Your Clouds*); **at the RSC** Chorus Leader (*Murder in the Cathedral*), Portia (*Merchant of Venice*), Princess of France (*Love's Labour's Lost*), Kate (*Taming of the Shrew*), Imogen (*Cymbeline*), Bertha (*Comrades*), Valeria (*Summerfolk*), Janet Morton (*Childhood Friend*); **at the National** Sybil Thorndike (*Tribute to the Lady*), Pegeen Mike (*Playboy of the Western World*), Ophelia (*Hamlet*), Jo (*Watch it Come Down*), Zenocrate (*Tamburlaine*), Claire (*Lavender Blue*); **tv** Pamela Redman (*Don't be Silly*), Hilda (*Eustace and Hilda*); **radio** Nora (*A Doll's House*); **at the National**, Nora (*Plough and the Stars*), Varya (*The Cherry Orchard*), Ismene (*The Woman*); **at the RSC** Rosalind (*As You Like It*); **radio** Tatyana (*Eugene Onegin*); **at the National** Titania (*Midsummer Night's Dream*), Principal Boy (*Cinderalla*); **at the RSC** wife in *La Ronde*; **at the National** June (*Way Upstream*); **tv** Lady Caroline (*Strangers and Brothers*), Frieda (*Dangerous*

Corner), Charlotte (*The Blue Dress*), Carol Sheridan (*Travelling Man*), Annie (*Murder of a Moderate Man*); **film** Dribb (*Young Sherlock Holmes*), Athene (*Clash of the Titans*), Beth Crawford (*Heat and Dust*), Leonora (*Good Soldier*), Adelaide (*The Sacrifice*); **West End** Clara (*I'm not Rappaport*); **at the Manchester Royal Exchange** Lady Kitty Twombley (*Cabinet Minister*); **at the National** Laura (*The Father*); **at Theatr Clwyd** Geraldine (*Strike up the Banns*); **at the RSC** Beatrice (*Much Ado*), Anna Arkadina (*Seagull*), Ella (*Curse of the Starving Class*); (**tv** Nardia/Marie (*A Few Short Journeys of the Heart*), Eva Kay (*Buddha of Suburbia*), Susanna (*Flying in the Branches*); **radio** Rachel, (*Exorcism*), Andromache (*King Priam*), wife to Dreyfus (*Prisoner of Honour*), Madre (*Daughters of Venice*), Kate (*Where the Boys Are*); **film** Aunt Rose (*The Krays*), Gwladys (*White Mischief*), psychiatrist (*Dream Demon*); **tv** Kate Phillips (*Chandler and Co.*), Molly Pargeter (*Summer's Lease*), Lady Russell (*Persuasion*), Elizabeth Serafin (*Landing on the Sun*).

Putative roles: Medea, Clytemnestra, Queen Margaret, Hedda Gabler, St. Joan, Coriolanus, George Sand.

As reader: Fifth Child.